THE
MEDICAL
SCHOOL
DEAN

REFLECTIONS & DIRECTIONS

D. Kay Clawson, MD
Emery A. Wilson, MD

McClanahan
Publishing House

International Standard Book Number 0-913383 63 5
Library of Congress Catalog Card Number 99 60111

Cover design and book layout by James Asher Graphics

Manufactured in the United States of America

All book order correspondence should be addressed to:

University of Kentucky, College of Medicine
MN150, Chandler Medical Center
Lexington, KY 40536-0298

McClanahan
Publishing House

The only difference between being dean and being dead is one "letter"

INDRODUCTION

"This is an important book with candid appraisals of the realities of the medical deanship from an array of our nation's best known and most thoughtful recent leaders. In an era when major leadership positions in academe change without the benefit in most instances of the exit interview which is a must for any other position, this book is an important beginning in what should be a continuing evaluation of leadership in our institutions by the people we have chosen to lead them. It should be on the reading list for all thoughtful and concerned members of the multiple constituencies that have a stake in the leadership of our nation's academic health science concerns. A job well done and a work long overdue."

Roger J. Bulger
President, Association of Academic Health Centers

"The book is great! That deaning is as much art as it is science is apparent from this new book about being a medical school dean. Contributors, all deans or former deans, are remarkably candid in sharing their experiences, advice and lessons learned during their years as administrators. Humorous statements, in terspersed throughout the book, enliven the text and teach readers the importance of not taking their responsibilities too seriously. This unique text makes a valuable contribution to the education of deans and future deans destined for careers in schools of medicine as well as other health professions disciplines and should be required reading for anyone contemplating a career in an academic health center."

Eleanor J. Sullivan, RN, Ph.D.
President, Sigma Theta Tau International
Former Dean, School of Nursing
University of Kansas

TABLE OF CONTENTS
CONTRIBUTORS

PREFACE

*T*his book is written out of concern for the "revolving door" of deanships in American medical schools with the average tenure of the dean now under three and one-half years. While it is clear that the strength of any medical school lies in the strength of its faculty and students, stability in leadership positions, particularly the deanship, is a critical factor in recruiting and retention of the best faculty and creating an environment for them to be most productive.

There are many excellent articles containing informative statistical information regarding dean turnover by type of school and region of the country.

In this book, we have reviewed the pertinent statistical information on dacanal longevity in Section I and have asked twenty-five individuals who have had a long tenure as deans or who are former deans who have gone on to higher administrative roles within universities or national academic organizations to provide their insight and reflections in Section II. In Section III, we have attempted to summarize the points made most often by these deans as being personal characteristics that contribute to success. We hope by doing so, it may be of help to young deans and particularly for individuals who may aspire to such a role to do self-assessments to determine if they have the attitudes and personality that will bode for success. We also talk about the critical issue of the transition of the deanship, knowing when and how to depart in the best interest of the school, but also urging faculty and other administrators to identify means by which deans can exit into other meaningful responsibilities in order to make medical deanships attractive to the most capable and prepared individuals.

A sense of humor appears to be a critical ingredient. Many of the deans have included stories, jokes or one-liners and we have left them as written. In addition, we have interspersed pertinent jokes or comments throughout the book (quotes and non-identified). We have done this for two reasons: 1) to provide a ready reference that individuals may pull from the book those jokes or quotes that are suitable for their use in a variety of speeches or conversations with faculty or administrators, and 2) we have dispersed them in such a way that we hope the reader may enjoy the jokes and anecdotes and, in the process absorb some value from the basic content of the book.

> We have chosen to separate the jokes and quotes, many of which we cannot identify a source to give credit, so that the reader will recognize that they are not part of the presentation of the contributors.

For Deans and faculty alike, attempting to accomplish our mission and goals is increasingly difficult - The following describes the situation today as we attempt to make change.

The Court of King George III
London, England

July 10, 1776

Mr. Thomas Jefferson
c/o The Continental Congress
Philadelphia, Pennsylvania

Dear Mr. Jefferson:

We have read your "Declaration of Independence" with great interest. Certainly, it represents a considerable undertaking, and many of your statements do merit serious consideration. Unfortunately, the Declaration as a whole fails to meet recently adopted specifications for proposals to the Crown, so we must return the document to you for further refinement. The questions which follow might assist you in your process of revision.

1. In your opening paragraph you use the phrase "the Laws of Nature and Nature's God." What are these laws? In what way are they the criteria on which you base your central arguments? Please document with citations from the recent literature.

2. In the same paragraph you refer to the "opinions of mankind." Whose polling data are you using? Without specific evidence, it seems to us the "opinions of mankind" are a matter of opinion.

3. You hold certain truths to be "self-evident." Could you please elaborate? If they are as evident as you claim, then it should not be difficult for you to locate the appropriate supporting statistics.

4. "Life, Liberty, and the Pursuit of Happiness" seem to be the goals of your proposal. These are not measurable goals. If you were to say that "among these is the ability to sustain an average life expectancy in six of the 13 colonies of at least 55 years, and to enable newspapers in the colonies to print news without outside interference, and to raise the average income of the colonists by 10 percent in the next 10 years," these could be measurable goals. Please clarify.

5. You state that "Whenever any Form of Government becomes destructive of these ends, it is the Right of the People to alter or to abolish it, and to institute a new Government... ." Have you weighed this assertion against all the alternatives? What are the trade-off considerations?

6. Your description of the existing situation is quite extensive. Such a long list of grievances should precede the statement of goals, not follow it. Your problem statement needs improvement.

7. Your strategy for achieving your goal is not developed at all. You state that the colonies "ought to be Free and Independent States" and that they are "Absolved from All Allegiance to the British Crown." Who or what must change to achieve this objective? In what way must they change? What specific steps will you take to overcome the resistance? How long will it take? We have found that a little foresight in these areas helps to prevent careless errors later on. How cost-effective are your strategies?

8. Who among the list of signatories will be responsible for implementing your strategy? Who conceived it? Who provided the theoretical research? Who will constitute the advisory committee? Please submit an organization chart and vitae of the principal investigators.

9. You must include an evaluation design. We have been requiring this since Queen Anne's War.

10. What impact will your problem have? Your failure to include any

assessment of this inspires little confidence in the long-range prospects of your undertaking.

11. Please submit a PERT diagram, an activity chart, an itemized budget, and a manpower utilization matrix.

We hope that these comments prove useful in revising your "Declaration of Independence." We welcome the submission of your revised proposal. Our due date for unsolicited proposals is July 31, 1776. Ten copies with original signatures will be required.

Sincerely,

Management Analyst to the British Crown

SECTION I
HISTORY

1

> *Success is a journey, not a destination.*
>
> Ben Sweetland

THE MEDICAL SCHOOL DEAN

David S. Greer, MD

THE MEDICAL SCHOOL

The origins of the modern American academic medical center are obscure but may be dated to the establishment of the Johns Hopkins Medical School and its hospital in 1893. Until the late nineteenth century, hospitals had for many centuries been institutions for the care and support of people who were ill, fragile, or dying, and thus unable to maintain themselves in the community; most were indigent and without family or other social support. The concept of the hospital as a place for the treatment, and perhaps cure, of diseases rather than a place to die was a late-nineteenth-century idea; and the giant conceptual step to the hospital as an educational institution was radical when the Johns Hopkins Medical School was established.

No one could possibly have envisioned in 1893 the evolution of the medical school-hospital partnership to the giant, complex, contemporary academic medical center. Indeed, more than a decade passed before others were emboldened to emulate the Johns Hopkins model, notably Columbia's College of Physicians and Surgeons (Presbyterian Hospital), the Harvard Medical School (Peter Bent Brigham Hospital), and Washington University Medical School (Barnes and St. Louis Children's Hospital), all of which were established in 1910. In each case, Johns Hopkins served as the model: the universities were granted the right to appoint the medical staff of the affiliated hospitals and to use the facility for teaching and research.

The affiliates in Boston, New York, and St. Louis served as catalysts; the establishment of teaching hospitals associated with medical schools accelerated rapidly. Hospitals, once adamantly opposed to medical teaching, flocked to the new paradigm; medical educators were astounded by the rapid acceptance of an idea that had been so staunchly resisted only a few years before. Many affiliations were created with private hospitals, but a large number were also established with public institutions. After publication of the Flexner report in 1910, failure to establish a teaching hospital contributed to the closure of many ambitious medical schools.

THE TEACHING HOSPITAL

The conceptual revolution that produced teaching hospitals would not have been possible without an equally revolutionary change in American medical education, which occurred simultaneously with and often anticipated the change in hospitals. American medical education until the late nineteenth century was almost exclusively the domain of private practitioners, serving as preceptors in an apprenticeship mode or as owners of for-profit medical schools, where they also constituted the faculty. With the growth of medical knowledge, a new class of doctors arose, full-time professors, and these assumed control of medical education and research. Private practitioners did not surrender control without a struggle, but, by the early twentieth century, the trend toward full-time academic faculty was apparent, and increasing numbers of enterprising academics became available to serve in the multiplying teaching hospitals.

During the first half of the twentieth century, medical school-teaching hospital relations expanded, but progress was evolutionary rather than revolutionary. By the 1920's, the task of institution-building in medical education had been completed, and the schools that had survived the "Flexnerian Revolution" had assumed their modern shape: scientifically based, hospital-connected organizations. But medical education before World War II remained a cottage industry. Full-time faculties, both basic science and clinical, grew gradually; in the 1940's they numbered only a few thousand. Employment arrangements were stable and centralized either in the schools or in the affiliated hospitals. Total school revenues nation-wide were minuscule. Rapid qualitative and quantitative change occurred in the post-World War II period; the contemporary medical center is the product of professional, social, and economic vectors of the past fifty years.

THE ADMINISTRATIVE STRUCTURE

In the early 1900's, the administrative structure of medical schools was informal. Authority lay in the hands of the deans who were, however, predominantly part-time administrators, continuing their involvement in teaching, research, and practice. As the schools grew in size and complexity, full-time deans became more commonplace, and the positions of assistant and associate deans were created at many schools. By the 1930's, deans frequently were unable to properly administer all aspects of the growing enterprise, and important duties were assigned to department chairs. Expanded hospital-based duties enlarged clinical departments that, in some cases, became as large as entire schools had once been.

After World War II, the rate of change in medical schools approached explosive proportions. The rapid pace of technological innovation and increasing consumer demand for specialized medical care resulted in accelerated enlargement and subspecialization of the clinical departments. The entry of federal and state governments into health care financing in 1965, through both Medicare and Medicaid, provided a financial stimulus to the growth of medical centers that was unprecedented; the rate of growth in the cost of medical services nationally rose from 3.2% in the seven years before Medicare to 7.9% annually in the five years afterward, and escalation of health care costs at a disproportionate rate has persisted (with some deceleration in the past few years). Since one man's costs are another man's profits, clinical departments experienced gigantic growth rates (Figure 1); in the past fifty years, these clinical departments have become powerful forces in the administration of medical schools.

Simultaneously, in the past half-century there has been a remarkable expansion of biomedical research fueled by an enormous infusion of federal funds. This expansion of research has further stimulated growth in faculty size, support personnel (technicians, research assistants, managers), and physical facilities. The research imperative has become a predominant focus of many medical schools, some would say to the detriment of the educational mission. Research and clinical responsibilities compete for resources and faculty time; scientists and clinicians have become contending forces within many institutions.

Finally, there has been an increase in curriculum experimentation in the past several decades. As the size of medical school classes

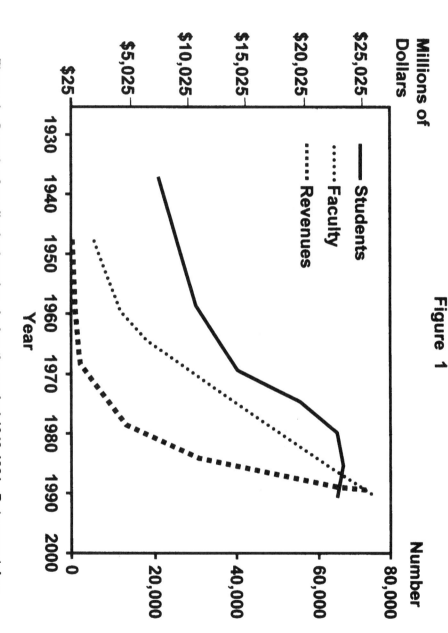

Figure 1

Figure 1. Growth of medical education during the period 1940-1991. Data were taken from J.R. Schofield's *New and Expanded Medical Schools: Mid-Century to the 1980s* (Jossey-Bass, 1984) and the AAMC Data Book, 1992.

has increased (Figure 1) and the complexity of the knowledge base has grown, established pedagogical methods have become inadequate. A crowded, highly structured curriculum taught in a passive fashion by an increasingly specialized faculty has lost coherence. Integration, "active" learning, greater flexibility, and the introduction of the medical humanities are the objectives of many of these attempts at curricular reform. Management of the curriculum has become a full-time job in most medical schools.

THE MODERN ERA

The modern medical school is a big business with yearly budgets in the tens and hundreds of millions of dollars and vast and intricate connections to the health care delivery system - itself in a dynamic (some would say chaotic) condition. The contemporary medical school produces a variety of "products" and encompasses a mission extending far beyond the walls of the ivory tower. Indeed, its scope and broad impact have fostered additional criticism, the accusation that medical education with its focus on research and specialized clinical care has lost touch with the needs of the community that supports it and is insufficiently involved in the maintenance of community health. In the past two decades, "community-based" medical schools have proliferated, in which the walls of the educational institutions veritably disappear and the educational-research mission expands into the community at large.

The medical school of the 1990s has a large, dispersed, and heterogeneous constituency. The demands on it are enormous, highly disparate, and sometimes conflicting. Medical student education, once the sole mission of medical schools, has become a minor player in the enterprise of the large academic medical center.

Large bureaucracies are obviously needed to oversee these vast, heterogeneous organizations. The "academic medical center" has emerged as the predominant organizational structure, with varying permeability of its boundaries. A variety of new administrative positions has evolved: vice presidents who oversee a cohort of health professional schools; hospital chief executive officers who administer the largest financial entity in most centers, the teaching hospital and its clinics; deans of medicine who may also serve as vice presidents or hospital CEOs; and armies of accountants, development officers (fund-raisers), trustees, elected officials, and others who constitute a mammoth, complex constituency.

THE FATE OF DEANS

In the midst of each of these vast medical centers sits a single person responsible for the academic quality of the medical school and the professional competence of the physicians it produces: the dean of medicine. The book *Leadership and Management in Academic Medicine* by Wilson and McLaughlin, 1984, is the most complete document to that time on the characteristics and longevity of deans and other academic administrators. Banaszak-Holl and Greer's studies, 1997, bring an update of trends and conditions to the present. The medical school dean is immersed in a multi-institutional bureaucracy encompassing numerous, often discordant, missions and priorities; the dean's task is somehow to bring this heterogeneous constituency together in joint academic endeavor, both education and research. It is not surprising that this task has become increasingly difficult in recent decades and that the position of dean has become tenuous and unstable. Stewarding the gargantuan medical center enterprise of the late twentieth century entails organizational challenges and leadership talents different from those of the early cottage indus-

---

[1] Wilson and McLaughlin have drawn up a daunting list of thirty constituencies that make demands on the medical school and its dean, including faculty, students, underrepresented minorities, university officials, alumni, parents of students, boards of trustees, affiliated hospitals, third-party payers, Medicare and Medicaid, medical center patients, donors, foundations, state legislators and governors, state higher education agencies, the Equal Employment Opportunity Commission, federal congressional representatives, the National Institutes of Health, the Department of Health and Human Services, local government, county and state medical societies, national associations and accrediting bodies, the Association of American Medical Colleges, unions, and news media.(Footnote Wilson and McLaughlin). It should therefore not be surprising that the turnover of medical school deans in the United States has been increasing in recent decades.

Table 1
Distribution of Tenures for All Deans* and Actual Deans 1940 through 1992

	1940 - 59	1960 - 79	1980 - 92	Total
All deans				
Years in office				
1-4	92 (44%)	187 (49%)	196 (73%)	475 (55%)
≥5	117 (56%)	196 (51%)	74 (27%)	387 (45%)
Total	209	383	270	862
Tenure average	6.7 years	5.8 years	3.5 years	5.3 years
SD	5.2 years	4.6 years	2.6 years	4.5 years
Still in office	0%	3%	43%	15%
Actual deans				
Years in office				
1-4	63 (35%)	125 (39%)	129 (64%)	317 (45%)
≥5	116 (65%)	196 (61%)	74 (36%)	386 (55%)
Total	179	321	203	703
Tenure average	7.6 years	6.6 years	4.1 years	6.2 years
SD	5.2 years	4.6 years	2.7 years	4.5 years
Still in office	0%	3%	50%	16%

*Includes interim appointments.

Table 2
Incidence of Acting / Interim Deans among New Hires, 1940-1989

Decade	All Schools		Old Schools		New Schools	
	No. of Acting	% of Deans Hired	No. of Acting	% of Deans Hired	No. of Acting	% of Deans Hired
1940-1949	25	23	25	23	*	*
1950-1959	15	15	15	15	*	*
1960-1969	37	23	37	26	0	0
1970-1979	69	31	48	33	21	27
1980-1989	73	32	48	32	25	33

*Not applicable, since new schools are defined as those established after 1959.

try days. Modern deans swim in a mind-boggling sea of constituencies and administrative relationships.[1] It should therefore not be surprising that the turnover of medical school deans in the United States has been increasing in recent decades.

THE TENURE OF DEANS

The average tenure of deans has decreased historically, (table 1) from an average of 6.7 years for deans starting during the period 1940 to 1959 to an average of only 3.5 years for deans starting in 1980 to 1992. Similarly, the percentage of deans in office for four years or less (i.e., not completing the common contractual or anticipated term) has increased over time, from 44% in 1940 to 1959, to 73% in 1980 to 1992, including all sitting deans. This trend toward an increasing number of short-term deans remains even when deans still in office are removed from the sample.

These trends persist no matter how one cuts the data: if "acting" deans are removed from the sample, the average tenure of deans declines from 7.6 years in 1940 to 1959, to 6.6 years in 1960 to 1979, to 4.2 years for deans starting since 1980. The percentage of these "actual" deans with tenures of four years or less also has increased in the last five decades, from 35% in 1940 to 1959, to 64% in 1980 to 1992. These statistically significant trends apply to both old schools and new schools (the cohort of schools established in the past three decades), to public and private schools.

In both old and new schools, the incidence of acting or interim deans has increased over time, although the 1950s had the fewest interim hires (table 2). In both the 1940s and the 1960s, 23% of deans were hired as acting or interim deans, compared with 15% of the deans hired in the 1950s; since then, new hires of acting or interim deans has risen progressively, to 31% in the 1970s and 32% in the 1980s. This institutional inability to make long-term commitments to leadership at times of transition is further evidence of administrative instability.

The frequency of dean tenures is not evenly distributed among medical schools. Some schools have had a disproportionately large number of deans with short tenures; other schools tend to have longer-tenured deans who have remained for ten years or more. The Banaszak-Holl and Greer study found that 14% of the schools had more than five deans with tenures of four years or less, whereas 13% of the schools had no dean with a tenure under five years.

Banaszak-Holl and Greer have suggested that organizational and environmental factors rather than the characteristics of the deans may be at the root of the turnover problem. Rebecca Levin and Michael Yedidia appear to have confirmed this hypothesis: in their study, schools experiencing a decline in resources after an era of abundance - often as a result of unprecedented competition in the clinical arena, schools sharing common ownership of the primary teaching hospital, and schools with larger numbers of faculty members tended to have shorter dean tenures and higher dean turnovers.

One may hypothesize that short tenures do not necessarily reflect failure but, rather, improved opportunities for deans to go on to larger roles or more attractive positions; or that the prior administrative experience of more recently appointed deans may be inadequate to prepare them for the dean's role. In a follow-up study of dean tenure designed to test these possibilities, Banaszak-Holl and Greer found, contrarily, that recently appointed deans have been more likely to have administrative experience, as chairs or lower-level administrators, than the earlier cohort. In addition, they found that the kinds of positions that deans took upon leaving office did not change historically. More attractive employment opportunities do not appear to be the reason for increased dean turnover in recent years.

ETIOLOGY AND PATHOGENESIS

The increasing turnovers of deans of medicine does not appear to be explainable on the basis of changes in the qualifications of the individuals or by progressively greater opportunities for deans upon leaving office. Other personal characteristics of deans, such as charisma or leadership skills, are also unlikely explanations for the increasing turnovers in recent decades; they probably play a role in a person's success in office, but there is no reason to expect that the prevalence of those characteristics has changed historically.

Organizational and environmental factors seem the most likely causes of increased dean turnovers. The clustering of long-term deans in some institutions, whereas other institutions seem to "eat up" deans, is consistent with this hypothesis. Further study is needed to identify the underlying operative organizational and environmental factors. In the management field, current research on people in leadership positions and those working in administration indicates that the institutional environment and the leader's ability to work within existing administrative situations are the key components associated with effective administration and long tenure.

CONCLUSION

The pervasive sense of vulnerability among American deans of medicine is supported by experience, both personal and national. Deans' tenures have become progressively shorter and less predictable in recent decades.

The causes of this phenomenon are multiple. Medical schools are now units of large, multi-institutional bureaucracies; deans no longer live in the splendid isolation of yesteryear. Medical schools have themselves grown extremely rapidly in size and complexity; they often are composed of multiple fiefdoms, with departmental and other power centers competing for dominance. Faculty mobility and market forces dilute institutional commitment; the dean is often the only - and lonely - advocate of the school's institutional priorities. The revenues of academic medical centers have exploded astronomically, and little of this increase is in direct support of education. And "money talks" in most contemporary academic medical centers. The predominance of clinical revenue shapes institutional priorities.

For most deans, situational control, authority, and influence have diminished, whereas responsibility has grown. When difficulties arise, the dean is the easiest and most visible target to attack; as has been said of the Pope, he has few "divisions." Removal of the dean makes it possible to avoid the unpleasantness often associated with addressing the realities of institutional pathology or environmental instability.

In 1992, the last year of the Banaszak-Holl and Greer study, 57% of the sitting deans of medicine in the United states had been in office four years or less; 26% of them were acting or interim deans. The Levin and Yedidia study confirmed that this trend persisted until 1995, the last year that data were available.

Short dean tenures are an organizational problem and also a personal problem for the deans. Continuity of administration and effective management relationships suffer. Short-tenured deans are limited in their ability to follow through on policy changes or to initiate long-term projects. Institutional instability feeds on itself, establishing conditions that foster greater numbers of short-tenured deans. Some institutions become "revolving doors," with an inordinately high prevalence of short- term deans. At a time of unprecedented turmoil in the health care delivery and educational systems, organizational stability is more important than ever. From both individual and organizational perspectives, the problem of instability in medical school leadership is in dire need of creative solutions.

REFERENCE:

Leadership and Management in Academic Medicine, Margorie Price Wilson, Kurtis P. McLaughlin, Association of American Medical Colleges, 1 Dupont Cr., Suite 200, Washington, D.C., 20036, Jossey-Bass, Inc.

Banaszak-Holl, Jane, PhD, and Greer, David S., M.D., Turnover of Deans of Medicine During Last Five Decades, *Academic Medicine*, January, 1994, Vol 69, pages 1-7.

Levin, Rebecca J. and Yedidia, Michael, Financial, Administrative and Organizational Factors Influencing Dean's Tenure, submitted for publication, Academic Medicine, June, 1998.

*P*erhaps the best known joke about deans is the one about "three letters." As the story goes, a new dean was being oriented to his office when the retiring dean told him that if he ever had a problem, he should consult the advice in one of the three letters he had prepared and left in his desk. Things went well for a while but before long the new dean developed a major problem with the faculty. Remembering his predecessor's advice he opened the first letter in his desk which said "Blame your predecessor." This he did and things seemed to go well for awhile until a second problem arose. The new dean consulted the second letter which said "Blame the University administration." Again, things began to improve only to turn worse later with another faculty uproar. He then opened the third letter which said, "Prepare three letters."

*A*t a recent national meeting where medical schools continued to be blamed for the lack of physicians in rural areas, one spokesman said, "In my next life, I want to be dean of a school of agriculture instead of medicine. Somehow, they never seem to blame the schools of agriculture for a drought."

SECTION II
REFLECTIONS

2

The sun will shine after every storm.

Emerson

REFLECTIONS ON ACADEMIC HEALTH SCIENCE LEADERSHIP

Lyn Behrens, MB, BS

$\mathcal{M}$y journey from July 1986, as a new school of medicine dean, to the present, as president of an academic health sciences center, has been one of ever-widening and exciting opportunities intermittently interrupted by unexpected and unwanted yet growth-facilitating challenges.

LIFE'S MOUNTAIN-TOP EXPERIENCES

• Addressing the freshmen students on their first day of classes. With unabated confidence and enthusiasm, they are eager to tackle the task of acquiring the knowledge and skills that will prepare them to serve humanity. They have yet to discover the effort and energy required to complete their professional training.

• Participating in their graduation four short years later. With faces wreathed in smiles, they confidently stride forward. With a firm handshake they receive the prized parchment that certifies their professional success. Applause swells from proud spouses, parents, siblings, friends, and faculty members. Then they are gone sailing forth to near and distant destinations to pursue graduate medical education and wider service. The toil of students and faculty members that led to this accomplishment is erased by the joy of their academic success.

• Sharing with researchers their moments of ecstasy. As scientific hypotheses are validated and new and more effective methods of diagnosis and treatment become reality, all have forgotten the uncertainties of funding sources and second-guessed decisions about resource allocation.

• Pausing to celebrate the completion of new facilities. Before you stands the edifice: a mass of steel and cement, gleaming glass, spotless paint, glowing bronze, unstained carpet, modern furniture, and immaculate landscaping. The donors are appropriately recognized and thanked, the dedication is invoked, the garlands of ribbons are cut, and for a few hours, days, and maybe even weeks, faculty members, staff, and students celebrate the convenience of the new facilities. Few know about the stress of sleepless nights involved in the struggle to complete the project's capital campaign.

DEATH VALLEYS OF LEADERSHIP

Occasionally, severe and overwhelming challenges arise. They are the "Death Valleys" of leadership. Discouragement and despair come when one's supreme and best efforts are clearly misdirected, misunderstood, misapplied, or miserably misrepresented.

• There are tough choices when unbalanced budgets necessitate downsizing, and when various and unforeseen circumstances necessitate the elimination of programs begun with enthusiasm but terminated in disappointment.

• There is mental turmoil when one must identify and implement the best of a number of poor options, any one of which will result in an undesirable outcome.

• There is personal pain when the dean tries to negotiate a cease-fire between parties in conflict but leadership is caught in the cross-fire and becomes a war casualty.

THE JOY OF PARTICIPATING

Nevertheless, for all the challenges, there is sheer joy in participating in such a noble calling. It is awesome to reflect on the impact made by schools of medicine and academic health centers on the well being of individuals, families, and our global community. In spite of the hurricane of change that currently batters health care and higher education and occupies so much of our attention, enormous satisfaction accrues from preparing the next generation of health professionals and scientists; from supporting investigators who passionately pursue basic and applied research; and from meeting the health care needs of local and regional communities, providing them with competent, comprehensive, and compassionate care.

With study and the retrospectroscope of time, each academic leader identifies professional and institutional success factors and detractors. My administrative years have been packed full of such learning. In addition, I have had to learn to blend my roles as a spouse and mother with the incessant demands of leadership. Some of these insights I have codified into a *"Personal Creed for Academic Leaders."* This creed does not presume to substitute for or to embellish the essential knowledge that can be gained from solid research on business and institutional success. Learning and applying such organizational knowledge is the responsibility of every academic leader. Rather, this personal creed invites introspection. It is a call to journey to the inner world of personhood; it is an invitation to care for and nurture one's own well-being. I share this creed in the hope that some would-be or new administrators might avoid some of the land mines that interrupt the accomplishment of the institutional mission; that they might more fully accomplish their professional goals; and that it might help to preserve and enhance personal wholeness.

A PERSONAL CREED FOR ACADEMIC LEADERS

I WILL

Live life fully - fulfilling my mission in life, celebrating my uniqueness, and identifying my strengths and weaknesses.

Excel by regularly setting professional and personal goals - acquiring the necessary knowledge and skills, removing identifiable barriers, and being flexible enough to grasp unexpected opportunities.

Achieve balance between my professional and personal lives - giving priority to my own health and well-being; nurturing my intellectual, physical, emotional, and spiritual dimensions; setting appropriate limits and living within my means.

Dare to dream, to be different, and to be a change-maker in the world.

Effectively communicate what I know and believe - being a good listener and involving others in shaping and translating the institutional vision.

Remember that time is life's most valuable resource - always using my time, and that of others, carefully and with accountability.

Seek the good of others, doing for them what I wish that they would do for me - valuing diversity and focusing on *"servant leadership."*

Hold myself to standards of excellence, reaching for my maximum potential - personally and professionally.

Incorporate values of compassion, integrity, justice, freedom, inclusion, impartiality, hopefulness, respect, self-control, and humility into the fabric of my life.

Persistently improve my performance - accepting full responsibility for my actions, learning from and not repeating my mistakes.

> *"The essence of leadership is that you have to have vision and articulate it on every occasion."*

3

> $\mathscr{A}$ constituent told his congressman, "Whatever you do, don't let the federal government take over my Medicare."
>
> ~
>
> *If you think health care is expensive now, wait until it's free.*

PERSONAL REFLECTIONS ON DEANING

L. Thompson Bowles, MD, PhD

$\mathcal{L}$eadership in a complex organization such as a medical center is a challenging and rewarding assignment that can be done well by people with brains, physical and emotional sturdiness, and skill in communication. It helps to have experience as a clinician, an educator, and an investigator so that problems faced in these areas of faculty endeavor are understood and the leader has credibility when decisions are made.

As is true of many other professions, running a medical center involves challenges that relate to time and place. The time of my experience ranged from 1975 to 1992, a period extending through an era in which the country began to suspect that we were producing too many doctors and spending too much on medical care. By 1992, we *knew* that we were producing too many doctors and spending too much money to do so. The money spent on Medicare was threatening to bankrupt that vital program. The place of my experience, the District of Columbia, was (and still is) an anomalous political jurisdiction, evolving from its status as the last U.S. mainland colony in 1975 to home rule, which by 1992 was proving to be dangerously ineffective.

DEANS AS CHEERLEADERS-MEDIATORS

With this description of time and place in mind, I can say that the dean's job at George Washington was fun, frustrating, and always challenging. Deaning is roughly one-third cheerleading, including fund raising; one-third fast gun, particularly dispute resolution; and one-third swimming in the sewer, largely conflict management. This last third occasionally feels like the full demand on one's effort. Building consensus among chairs and faculty members is hard work but a necessary effort even when impossible. When things are going well, wise deans credit others. When something goes badly, deans should accept responsibility and blame without excuse. It is helpful for deans to appear upbeat and optimistic. Even when they are discouraged, leaders must communicate a positive outlook for the institution. Faculty members and university officials must recognize their deans as believers in the mission of the medical center. When leaders are discouraged and communicate such feelings, the morale of faculty members will suffer, and energy and creativity will suffer as well.

Conflict management is a constant presence in the professional existence of all deans. A certain amount of jawboning with the disputing parties sometimes decreases the angst. Ultimately, however, in many issues, talk and consensus building go only so far. Some problems are basically unsolvable, even some that need solutions. In those instances, deans must make the call with little support. These are the times when general trust and faith in the dean are essential. The skills of deans in keeping people focused on their work are necessary in these situations so that critical energy is not diverted into plots and sabotage. In making decisions, it is important that deans not be too dependent on their jobs, because self-serving and protective decisions are quickly perceived and virtually guarantee that plots will be developed to exploit fear of losing the job.

DEANS AS LEADERS

Deans are the leaders of special and important communities, usually involving thousands of people, hundreds of millions of dollars each year, and the medical care of thousands of people annually. In many institutions, the medical center earns and spends more than half of a large university's budget. The medical center may be the largest employer in town, especially if a hospital is part of the center.

Deans need a vision of the medical center's place in the community, the country, and the world. They need a plan to make the vision happen and the communication skills to assure that the community, the university administration, and the faculty members support the vision and the plan. The fun of deaning is shepherding the plan and seeing its details materialize. To be sure, some zigging and zagging are necessary as circumstances change, old players leave, and new ones arrive, but the plan's overall progress should be clear as the vision begins to emerge.

When resources cannot match demand or even need, their allocation becomes critical. Deans are often the final arbiters in directing important dollars, space, and faculty positions. Much thought should accompany the assignment of these resources. There are inevitably winners and losers when these decisions are made. Be assured, the losers will remember their loss. The gratitude of the winners will last only until the next assignment of resources. Making decisions makes enemies. To blunt the anger and discouragement that follow the unfulfilled aspirations of department chairs and center directors, there must be sound reason and fairness behind all decisions. Those disappointed must at least understand the basis of an undesired decision and recognize its connection to the plan and the vision. Although there will continue to be disagreement about the wisdom of some actions, the need for revenge by those disappointed will be moderated somewhat by understanding. It is essential that the powerful chairs, the largest money generators, the most successful investigators, and the most renowned as well as the mainstream faculty members know that their dean is unequivocally committed to the institution and makes decisions for the good of the organization as a whole.

Wise deans will cultivate the good will and respect of their university presidents and members of the Board of Trustees. The trust and faith of these people in the leader of the medical center leader is often critical when a serious conflict arises between the dean and some powerful members of the faculty. Such conflicts are inevitable, even if, one hopes, they are infrequent.

Wise deans will befriend as many department chairs and center directors as possible. Conflicts among chairs are inevitable, as are conflicts between chairs and deans. Strong friendships between deans and individual chairs allow trust to moderate what will sometimes be seen as an adverse action by the dean. It helps to be well liked and known as fair and honest, particularly when decanal actions affect some departments adversely. Deans need the trust and good will of the chairs individually and collectively to withstand the discontent that follows tough decisions. I used to tell faculty members that every decision I made invariably irritated one-third of them. After making three decisions a day, I had alienated everyone in the place. This kind of humor got me through some difficult periods.

Deans should cultivate an open and respectful relationship

with the students. Student leaders, although often vocal, militant, and naive, are usually bright, forward-thinking, and possessed of excellent values. Interacting with student leaders and student groups helps deans stay close to the concerns and aspirations of these groups. Deans learn a good deal about the strengths and weaknesses of their faculty members and educational programs from students. Even if student recommendations are frequently impractical or impossible, time spent with the student body to explain the medical center's stance on policy and other issues is well worth the commitment.

DEANING IS POLITICS

Finally, it is helpful if deans enjoy the political rough-and-tumble of the job. I entered the dean's office from a career in surgery where most patients do well and are grateful for the surgeon's efforts on their behalf. Deaning does not provide the daily satisfaction of patient care. Positive feedback is limited. Many excellent faculty members, including department chairs, are good at what they do and yet are ineffective at deaning. Keeping divergent forces working together is a special challenge and requires a special skill. The dean must keep the internal forces together while engaging the diverse and complex forces of the external community. From thence comes the agony and the ecstasy of deaning. The thrill of performing well is extremely rewarding. Hardships and challenges are attached to any meaningful work and are well worth the bearing by deans, at least for those suited to the challenge. To help develop and maintain an environment in which bright people can learn, teach, investigate, and practice medicine is one of the highest callings I can imagine. I would not trade a day of the experience. Well, not many days, anyway.

*C*harles Dickens wrote that these are the best of times and the worst of times. There are days when I think Dickens was only half right.

~

*T*he trick is to keep the 100 faculty members who dislike you from talking to the other 400 who are undecided.

4

> *As Mark Twain said about Wagner's music,*
> *"It's not as bad as it sounds."*

THE ROLE OF A DEAN:
ADVICE FOR THE SEARCH COMMITTEE

George T. Bryan, MD

*W*hat are the qualifications for being a dean? Unfortunately, there is no short list of such qualifications, and the long lists are general and open to much interpretation. The best I can do is to provide a picture of the position, as I see it.

The qualifications for leadership in academic health centers were a prominent part of the Josiah Macy, Jr., Foundation's "Report of the Commission for the Study of the Governance of the Academic Medical Center" (not dated but followed a 1967 Macy Conference), which examined governance in ten selected academic centers. The study was conducted by a dozen leaders of academic institutions. The following statements were made:

"In addition to the qualities of leadership required to initiate and implement policies, the dean of a school of medicine must have the capacity to coordinate and keep in balance the numerous and often conflicting elements that constitute such a complex institution. Furthermore, he is the one ultimately responsible for assembling the resources, human and physical, necessary to carry out its mission. To fill this role he must have the capacity to derive satisfaction from the achievements of others whom he has aided and supported, directly or indirectly." The report adds that "experience and demonstrated achievement in teaching, research and administration is highly desirable," and that "under current conditions, stamina and vitality are necessary." I agree that all of these qualities are highly desirable in a dean.

More than a decade ago, Wilson and McLaughlin, in the 1984 AAMC publication "Leadership and Management in Academic Medicine," devoted a chapter to analyzing the role of the dean and the characteristics sought by search committees. Although there have been dramatic changes in academic medicine since that time, their analysis is fundamental and provides a sound basis for searches in the late nineties.

You might consider applicants for the deanship in relationship to their levels of skill in managerial tasks. Mintzberg[1] divided managerial roles into three primary classes: interpersonal, informational, and decisional. The interpersonal role includes that of figurehead, leader, and liaison with other groups, both inside and outside the university. Informational roles include serving as the "nerve center," as disseminator of information and as spokesperson for the school. The decisional roles include entrepreneurship, handling disturbances, allocating resources and negotiating. I have adapted Mintzberg's description of these roles to apply to deanships and have examined my appointment book for an estimate of how one dean allocated his time among them.

THE INTERPERSONAL ROLES:

Interpersonal roles focus on interpersonal contact and derive from the authority and status of the title "dean" or "vice president."

Figurehead: As the "legal" or vested authorities for their schools, deans must preside at ceremonial events, meet certain visitors, meet site-visit teams, sign documents, and make themselves available to representatives from the public, the donor constituency, and the alumni who believe that the only way to get something done is to get to the top. For example, deans must meet foreign deans and scientists, chair meetings of the faculty members, and attend meetings of development boards, regents, and legislative committees. Deans must be present at community fund-raising events that relate in some way to the school. Routine documents that have been thoroughly reviewed by staff (and require no thought on the deans' part) must be signed. Deans must introduce meetings and continuing education functions as spokesperson for the institution.

Leader: Leadership is a part of almost all activities of deans. When proposing or defining new directions for their schools and when reinforcing existing directions, deans are exercising leadership. When responding to questions from subordinates or alumni, when asking questions of subordinates or staff, when encouraging or discouraging activities in the school, deans are providing clues about their values and the directions that they wish to sanction to faculty members and staff. This is the heart of the role of dean.

Liaison: For deans, there are two distinct categories of *liaison* activity. The first encompasses the vast network of personal and professional acquaintances that deans have developed throughout previous professional careers and those of a similar quality that will be developed during their tenure as dean. These acquaintances might include previous deans in this school or in other schools, former chairs, and colleagues on various boards and councils of professional and scientific organizations. Helpful but less likely to be considered would be associates from the business and managerial world outside of medicine, as these would bring perspectives not readily available to the dean of a medical school. The second category includes the more formal organizational relationships that require deans to serve as liaisons for the benefit of the school. Examples of these relationships include organized medical groups such as the county, state, and national medical societies, state medical licensing boards, state and national research advocacy groups, the local chamber of commerce, and the Association of American Medical Colleges and its Council of Deans.

THE INFORMATIONAL ROLES:

Informational roles refer primarily to receiving, processing, and transmitting information when deans are a critical "node" in deciding what is important and timely for the school and its constituents.

Nerve Center: Because deans are connected in one way or another with every member of their schools, they are recipients of vast amounts of information and have a broad perspective on issues within and outside the organization. Thus, filtering and integrating this huge quantity of information (some factual, some contextual, some outright rumor) and deciding whether to pass it on to others becomes an important role for the dean. Much of this information is "soft," word-of-mouth, unsubstantiated, and of unknown origin, but trends become important matters for deans to consider. Trends may indicate that deans need to take specific steps to flesh out the information by direct inquiry in strategic parts of the organization or elsewhere. But in sum, deans will be responsible for whether the "soft" information deserves consideration for the sake of their schools. For example, at a local social gathering a staff member may hear of an impending resignation. Certainly it is only rumor at this stage, but if strategic moves are being contemplated that involve this person, deans needs current and accurate information. Thus, deans constantly receive and provide information in a thoughtful way to further the work of the school while diminishing the anxiety of its constituents.

Disseminator: The transmission of both *factual* and *value-laden* information is a necessary part of the role of dean. Thus, deans transmit matters and issues important to the parent university, the governing body, outside constituencies, government agencies, and the health science center to faculty members, staff, and students as appropriate. For example, if an important trend such as school and hospital mergers is taking place around the country, the deans' perspectives on the trend and its implications for their schools are important information issues for staff, faculty members, and others within the schools. If National Institutes of Health appropriations are changing, then the deans' perspectives on how these changes will affect their schools are critical for maintaining morale, enthusiasm, and dedication to the scientific enterprise of the organization. The individual worries of one or two department chairs may merit open discussion at an executive committee meeting, or more wisely may be ignored in formal discussions and dealt with individually. Deans integrate the values that they espouse with the transmission of factual information within the organization.

Spokesperson: In the role of spokesperson, deans transmit information for or on behalf of their schools. Speaking for the school at formal site-visit evaluations by outside agencies such as scientific organizations, certification bodies, accrediting bodies, and foundations, deans present their schools to outside agencies and constituencies. Accomplishments, measures of effectiveness, fiscal matters, educational innovations, and needs are all transmitted to others on behalf of the school in the best light and from the perspective of its highest authority. The transmission of values and factual information is important and can only be accomplished with the imprimatur of the dean.

THE DECISIONAL ROLES

Decisional roles are those most often discussed by faculty members and students. "If only the dean would . . ." is a phrase repeated again and again by faculty members and staff. Yet the time devoted to decisional roles is often disproportionately less than that devoted to the interpersonal and informational roles discussed above. Decisional roles derive from the vested authority of deans and may be delegated, but are always the responsibility of the dean.

Entrepreneur: Initiating projects or changes in the function or structure of the school requires creative thought and strategic planning and implementation. Deans may choose to lead and supervise such change in a direct way, may delegate all aspects and the authority for implementation to someone else, or may delegate the development phase while withholding final approval authority. Deans may be involved in dozens of such projects at once. An important educational change, new directions in the health care program, a new research program, and a community outreach endeavor may all be underway at once, with varying degrees of personal involvement by the dean. If the dean's professional strengths are in research, the patient care and educational initiatives may by delegated to others with the new research program managed directly by the dean. It is most important to remember that this area of the dean's involvement is crucial to innovation and improvement in the school's programs, and that all other roles erode the dean's time, attention, and effort in the *entrepreneur* role.

Disturbance Handler: Deans are frequently the final arbiters or decision makers in matters of dispute within their schools. This function includes student discipline and academic matters, interpersonal issues between faculty members, outside threats to the function or the very existence of the school, and interdepartmental and inter-programmatic issues. With the overall perspective of the school, its roles in society, and the external and internal issues involved, the dean has a special place in the management of disturbances that affect the school. This role is costly in terms of time, effort, and, frequently, political capital. This role can rarely be anticipated and is always an interruption to the dean's scheduled activities. Thus, it is also an annoyance in terms of distraction and is usually not met with the same enthusiasm as are other roles. It is part of the job, however, and like other roles must be placed in perspective relative to the overall require-ments of the school. In medical matters, turf issues abound. Which department has the support of the school in developing a new pro-gram that is interdisciplinary in nature? Which surgical discipline has priority for scarce operating room time? Will the legislature direct an unwelcome curricular change? The list is never-ending, and deans must develop the ability to deal with such interruptions with a high degree of equanimity.

Resource Allocator: Deans control at least three precious and critical resources for the school. Although space and money are usual-ly thought of when "resources" are mentioned, time is equally impor-tant. The dean's time and energy are the first of these resources that must be actively allocated. The time spent on entrepreneurial activi-ties, for example, makes an important statement about the knowledge and experience of the dean, and the commitment of time also speaks volumes to the constituencies within and outside the school. The other "time" that must be managed by the dean is the time and effort of the staff and faculty. By the appointment and charging of commit-tees and task forces, as well as the requirement for measurable perfor-mance on matters of importance to the school, deans manage this pre-cious resource.

The second element of resource management involves the allocation of space to functions of the school. There never is enough space, and the location and quality are rarely optimal. The active man-agement of space and its use defines the priorities of the school as seen by the dean.

Finally, the allocation of fiscal resources, and especially their reallocation when situations change, is a primary role of deans. In general, a budgeting system is used as the basis for annual or biennial program functions, and deans and their staffs reallocate funding as necessary during the budget period. Resource allocation decisions by deans are interrelated. The commitment of the dean's time signifies priority and the expectation that faculty time, school space, and money will be forthcoming. Thus, embarking on a program requires careful thought and planning, because the initial overt commitment of the dean's own time and effort will affect perceptions of resource allocation. There must be devices to provide a framework for *ad hoc* resource allocation decisions, but the critical matter is that there be some conceptual structure against which to test individual decisions as they arise.

Negotiator: As *negotiator* for their schools, deans trade resources within or outside the school, including money, space, the time of faculty members and staff, and their own time, influence, and commitment. Within complex health science centers, compromises must always be made between competing priorities at certain points in time. As the single *authority* for their schools, deans or their designees are the only ones who can negotiate resources with the overall view and vision of the school in mind.

With these categories in mind, I analyzed retrospectively my own appointment books for a spring and fall month for each of three years (1992 through 1994). The results are displayed in Table I and Figure I . The great surprise to me was the preponderance of scheduled time in interpersonal roles and the relatively small percentage of scheduled time in "disturbance handler" activity. Perhaps this discrepancy came about because I enjoyed working with people staff, department chairs, faculty members, and students in a leadership role, but thoroughly disliked those same interactions when dealing with conflicts of various types.

Other deans will allocate their scheduled time differently, depending on their roles in the academic medical center and their work with outside organizations. However, if interpersonal roles are so

Table 1
SUMMARY of APPOINTMENTS and MEETINGS

	INTERPERSONAL			INFORMATIONAL				RESOURCE		
	Figurehead	Leader	Liaison	Nerve Center	Disseminator	Spokesperson	Entrepreneur	Disturbance Handler	Resource	Negotiator
Feb-92	22	33	24	1	0	6	2	9	16	0
Apr-93	23	38	42	2	0	1		4	3	0
Mar-94	28	63	11	6	0	39	10	6	4	0
Sep-92	15	35	25	4	0	1	1	12	12	0
Nov-93	32	49	57		0	13	1	11	12	0
Oct-94	23	57	31	2	0	13	2	8	8	0
TOTAL HRS.	143	275	190	15	0	73	16	50	55	0
% of Total	18%	34%	23%	2%	0%	9%	2%	6%	7%	0%
% of Role	74%			11%				15%		

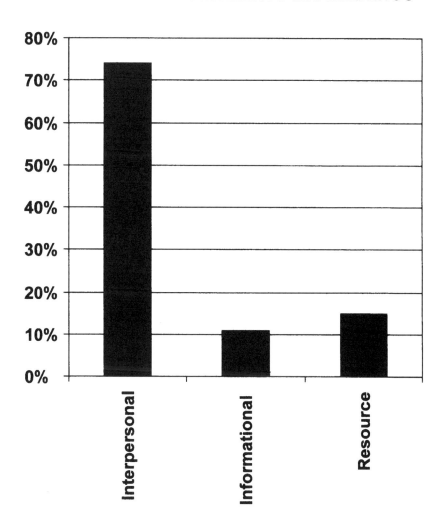

Figure 1
SUMMARY of APPOINTMENTS and MEETINGS

dominant in the dean's job, clearly <u>interpersonal skills are essential</u> for success.

Deans are constantly in the position of *interpreting* issues and potential decisions between two divergent organizational functions in the school. The position of dean is hierarchical by the terms of employment: that is, deans have delegated authority for their schools and for all activities emanating therefrom. In US medical schools, deans may serve a fixed term with renewal options or may serve "at the pleasure of" a higher university official or board. The work of the school is accomplished through the individual and group activities of its professional staff, the faculty members. Professional organizations are collegial in nature and thus exhibit the antithesis of hierarchy in their decisions and actions. The process of interpretation determines whether deans assign hierarchical or collegial methods in managing the functions of the school. For example, deans may believe that an important curricular revision is needed to improve students' education. It is possible to almost single-handedly impose curricular reform, but the resentment by faculty members may be enormous and thus the implementation flawed. On the other hand, if deans express their visions for a future educational program and then set the faculty members to examining and ultimately recommending changes, the process has become collegial, has supported the need for professionals to be relatively free from hierarchy, and has developed the participation of faculty members in the new curriculum.

Hierarchical authority is not the source of power in professional organizations (Feldmen)[2]. Hierarchical authority must have the *good will* of the professional staff so that administrative decisions by deans will at least be tolerated, if not actively supported. Thus, deans have enormous authority by virtue of title, but that authority must be supported by a significant measure of *good will* among their colleagues on the faculty. This *good will* must be earned by demonstrating sensitivity to academic issues and to those administrative decisions that are better taken after advice and counsel from faculty members.

As *interpreters,* deans must carefully judge which path to take when issues and decisions are not clearly in either the collegial or the hierarchical domain. Obtaining faculty members' support for hierarchical decisions (particularly if these decisions are not popular) draws on the *good will* that deans have developed by supporting the collegial domain.

Deans become the focal point for several competing forces within their schools, their universities, the medical profession, and other constituencies. Deans are always in the middle. Although deans are the chief academic officers of their school, they serve middle-management roles in the university and in other hierarchical relationships. Oshry[3] discusses three conditions in a managerial hierarchy: "topness," "middleness," and "bottomness." In my view, deans experience "topness" rarely, "bottomness" more frequently, and "middleness" almost constantly. For example, they are in the middle of situations involving clinical faculty versus the hospital management, students versus the student affairs office, and department chairs versus faculty members or students. The list is endless. Recognition of "middleness" in the dean's role and demonstrated skill and comfort in dealing with this situation are important qualities to seek in a dean.

Finally, although these thoughts have not identified nearly all of the qualities important for a dean, I must emphasize the most important qualities of all: integrity, both personal and intellectual, and the highest of ethical standards. These qualities are absolute requirements that provide the basis of trust that must prevail if the medical school is to thrive.

REFERENCES

1. Mintzberg, Henry. The Manager's Job: Folklore and Fact. Harvard Business Review. 19980; March-April: 163-176

2, Feldman, Steven P. The Crossroads of Interpretation: Administration in Professional Organization. Human Organization. 1987; 46: 95-102

3. Oshry, Barry. Middles of the World, Integrate! Boston: Power and Systems Training, Inc. 1982.

A man can succeed at anything as long as he sets his goals low enough.

~

*Q*uality is never an accident; it is always the result of high intention, sincere effort, intelligent direction, and skillful execution.

5

> *According to the faculty, Thomas Jefferson did not go far enough when he wrote the Declaration of Independence. The unalienable rights for faculty are life, liberty, pursuit of happiness, space and tenure.*

THIRTEEN YEARS OF DEANING
LESSONS LEARNED, AND A FEW RELEARNED

Lester R. Bryant, MD, ScD

*N*othing that I observed about the deans in the institutions where I trained and began my academic career inspired me to consider seeking a deanship. Instead, my inspiration for a leadership position came from observing strong department chairs who seemed to have the ideal opportunity to be excellent physicians, dynamic teachers, and "power brokers" if they shared a common vision. This feeling was reinforced during my first years as the founding chair in surgery at a new medical school, and I was completely disinterested in the first several attempts to nominate me for deanships.

It was a smooth-talking friend serving as a member of the dean search committee at another medical school who overcame my resistance to the risk of being a dean candidate. I refer to "risk" because I shared the view of many of my contemporaries who saw deans as people with a high likelihood of serving a short sentence and then needing special kinds of appointments to fill out the remaining years of their careers.

During the weeks that passed after I became a dean nominee, I came across a publication from the AAMC that reported on a survey of dean search committees. The results suggested that I had little chance of being selected since I was a surgeon, was an outside candidate, and would be 55 years of age at my next birthday. All of these factors seemed to be out of favor with search committees. Besides, the more I read about the super-human qualifications required by effective deans, the more I was tempted to withdraw. At first, it escaped my attention that most of the authors of these authoritative pieces had never been dean of a medical school.

For the personal sense of accomplishment that deaning has brought me, I will be forever grateful to the persistence of a few close friends, and especially to the dynamic president of the institution where I was subsequently appointed to the position of Vice President for Health Affairs and Dean of the School of Medicine. The encouragement of the friends to persist as a candidate and the open style of the president convinced me that the basic skills of a successful department chair could be leveraged into the tools needed for an effective deanship.

LEADING A MEDICAL SCHOOL

Now in my thirteenth year as a dean (at two medical schools), I will say without hesitation that the position has been rewarding and worth the total commitment required. Although I will comment later about important other qualifications needed to lead a medical school or academic medical center, in my opinion the two most important requirements are *integrity* and a *willingness to take risks.*

Being truthful is a fundamental leadership trait that seemingly needs no explanation. However, the deanship places a person into numerous situations in which it is tempting to cross your fingers behind your back while dealing with stressful situations. Even when it is publicly embarrassing to admit a bad decision, or to having inadequate experience to solve a complex situation, the dean's integrity must not become an issue. Over the years of my service, there have been many instances in which difficult situations have been resolved, or the breakdown of important negotiations has been averted, when one or more of the involved principals admitted that it was the trust that they had in the dean that allowed continued progress.

Perhaps *risk-taking* is easier for a dean whose career has been developed through a surgical discipline, but I believe it is a basic personality characteristic that can make the difference between comfort and misery in the dean's office. The dean must aggressively work at being informed, because being informed allows decisions to be made that best position the institution for the future. Some decisions will seem radical and will go counter to the "safe" alternative. For me, the greatest rewards of the deanship have come from the greatest risks, and I have strongly encouraged my colleagues to engage in risk-taking, even while acknowledging that occasional failures will occur. Related to risk taking, however, is the important quality of being *willing to change a decision* or an opinion without a feeling of lessened authority. Early in my own career, I began to realize that within the administrative bureaucracy of universities there are several levels of authority that seem to function primarily to stop initiatives. From this observation, I evolved one of the most important tenets of my own philosophy about risk-taking. That tenet is, "Don't ask!" Whether as a faculty member, a chair, or a dean, one is frequently presented with opportunities to take the initiative. You should do so with complete confidence that there are authorities "up the line" who can be counted on to apply the brakes if they see a risk to themselves. However, I have become convinced that many projects will get to the point of critical momentum without hindrance by the simple device of not asking for permission to proceed.

Another form of risk-taking is a willingness to constantly acknowledge the contributions of others for the success of the enterprise. Deans often are asked to comment at public functions without prior opportunity to prepare their remarks. This is often an opportunity to speak what is in your heart and to praise the efforts of others. I continue to be fascinated by the difficulty that many of my high-ranking peers have in these situations. They seem to feel that praise for others would come at their own expense.

> *There is no limit to what can be accomplished if we don't mind who gets the credit.* Robert Woodruff

EFFECTIVE LEADERSHIP

This discussion is really about leadership and the dean's perception of what constitutes effective leadership. I still have to remind myself that this is why I am paid a very generous salary and provided with many perks. Anger, frustration, and loneliness are among several emotions that a leader experiences on a regular basis. It is vitally important to be able to share these feelings with a very small circle of trusted colleagues, including one's spouse. But it is equally important to keep these brief disturbances in perspective so that the more encouraging emotions of *optimism*, *enthusiasm*, and *confidence* are the qualities seen by the constituencies being led.

Another characteristic of some university structures is the

unfortunate capacity to allow accountability to be replaced by anonymity. In developing a leadership team to administer an academic medical center, it is critical to require those who sit at the leadership table to accept accountability and standards of performance as requisites for membership. A corollary to accountability is the awareness that firmness and determination, two critical factors in leadership success, must never evolve into arrogance.

THE IMPACT OF HEALTH CARE REFORM

The present decade, with its complex issues of health care reform, has forced medical school deans to develop skills and strategies different from those characteristic of the academic medical centers in which we developed our early careers. We have had to call on our faculty members and staff to simultaneously maintain the integrity of the academic enterprise and to increasingly and aggressively compete in the health care market. Simply stated, I have been amazed at how well my own group has responded! Together, we have acquired the business acumen that we needed to compete successfully for managed care contracts, and we have become attractive partners so that we could participate in the health care consolidation that is sweeping across this nation. Unfortunately, the downside of this quickened pace has been a widening of the gap between effective and ineffective leaders, and between productive faculty members and those who refuse to change.

> *A managed care executive died and went to heaven. After finding out what he did on earth, St. Peter said he could be admitted ... but only for a three-day stay.*

DISAPPOINTMENTS

It is this unintended consequence of current academic life that reminds me of my disappointments. Although my authority as CEO of our health system provides considerable flexibility, I have not been able to adequately reward our greatest achievers because of university customs and regulations that protect mediocrity. I acknowledge the harshness of the term that I apply to those few noncontributing faculty who are allowed to consume resources at others' expense: "Academic Welfare Recipients." The failure to motivate these people to greater productivity has to be counted against my record.

Several disappointments have been associated with the selection of people for leadership positions. Some people will grow in their new positions with relatively little help; for others, appropriate mentoring increases their chances for success. I accept at least part of the blame for failure to provide the time and energy to help several talented people who could not achieve their potential without timely personal guidance from the dean.

STRATEGIES FOR ADMINISTRATORS

What are the important strategies that a dean should share with newly appointed chairs or directors? In addition to the leadership attributes already discussed, I suggest five strategies to those who have recently accepted significant responsibility.

- Keep ahead of your constituencies with creativeness and innovation.
- Offer assistance and guidance that will enhance the long-term prospects for the group.
- Focus on outcomes of clinical care, training, and research.
- Constantly seek to eliminate unproductive effort or divisive activities within the group.
- Seek alliances and partnerships that will enhance growth and productivity.

KNOWING WHEN AND HOW TO DEPART

Any consideration of deaning should include some helpful information or advice about leaving the deanship. Preferably, deans should leave at their own volition rather than as the result of actions taken by others. Part of the responsibility of deans is to acknowledge that they might leave the office with little notice regardless of the precipitating event. Therefore, it is important to institutional progress that a dean develop a "transition strategy". By this I mean that the dean should groom someone who is kept informed about and involved in important plans and strategies, and who is respected by the other leaders and by the hierarchy through which the dean reports. Further, if the institution is governed by some type of executive council, the dean should assure that the council is fully involved with the responsibilities of governance and serves as a truly representative body rather than as a collection of "turf protectors."

Finally, deans should try to reasonably estimate that date at which time they can gracefully acknowledge that another person can provide a new burst of energy, just as happens when the baton is handed off in a relay race.

A ship was on the high seas when the captain noticed a light far in the distance rapidly approaching. The captain sent the following message, "We are on the same course. Change course 15 degrees starboard immediately." Moments later he received a reply, "Negative. Suggest you change course 15 degrees port." The captain repeated his message, "I am an American destroyer. Change course 15 degrees starboard." Again, the reply was received, "Impossible, suggest you change course 15 degrees port." The irate captain was now adamant in his message, "I am the captain of an American destroyer. I demand you change course 15 degrees immediately." Moments later he received another reply, "You change course. I am a light house."

6

> ## Chinese Proverb
>
> *Tell me, I'll forget*
> *Show me and I may not remember*
> *Involve me and I'll understand.*
>
>
>
> *You never get a second chance at a first impression.*

ADMINISTRATION
IN AN
ACADEMIC MEDICAL CENTER

D. Kay Clawson, MD

$\mathcal{A}$fter more than thirty-six years as an administrator on a variety of levels in an academic medical center, I am convinced that the dean of the school of medicine has the most difficult of all positions. The organizational relationships and the institutional culture can make the position more or less demanding. However, the dean, being subservient to a board of lay people, a president, and often a vice president, who for the most part expect the dean to be a manager in the traditional hierarchical sense, and interfacing daily with faculty members, who expect and indeed demand a collegial style of management, can, in the best of times, result in some frictions and frustrations and, in more difficult times, make the job impossible. Tomes have been written on leadership and management, expounding detailed theories on the science behind successful companies, institutions, and, indeed, medical centers. Yet in practice, many of the most successful leaders and managers have never taken courses and certainly have never mastered the many theories advocated by leading authors on the subject. I have carefully noted the characteristics of those administrators who have had long, successful careers and those whose careers were shortened by adversity, disillusionment, and a decision to leave management to others. The list includes those things I did well when I was most successful and also explains why I had difficulty at times in carrying out my responsibilities in the manner that was expected of me and that I expected of myself. With the exception of the first item, these notes are presented below in no particular order as to judgment of more or less importance.

BEING LUCKY

It doesn't take many talents or skills to be a successful dean or other administrator and at times even to be loved in times of plenty. When an institution is growing and space and financial resources seem to be more than adequate, even some personality defects can be over looked. When resources are scarce or the political climate around and within the institution is not likely to be productive of new resources, the best administrators may find their time in position short-lived.

Incoming deans or vice presidents should choose the institution carefully and above all be careful when faculty members, staff, or other administrators blame the most recent incumbent for failures. Although the individual can influence the timing and choice of positions, it still is important to be lucky.

CHOOSING GOOD PEOPLE AND DELEGATING AUTHORITY

Choosing good people is more easily said than done. One always inherits staff from a predecessor, and determining which of those can be trusted and can accept and use delegated authority wisely and which must be replaced before one's own image is tainted is the most difficult task. The times when I have acted quickly in making needed changes within the administrative staff account for most of my successes. The times when for whatever reasons I accepted incumbents in key positions who were either over their heads in the responsibilities assigned to them or who could not be trusted with delegated authority account for most of my administrative failures. Although often forgotten, the person most key to one's administrative success will probably be the administrative assistant or personal secretary, who by personality and organization sets the tone of the administration, making the dean available when necessary, protecting the dean to some degree, but always presenting the administration as being kind, concerned, and helpful. Such an assistant may be worth more than the dean.

When you hire people who are smarter than you are, you prove you are smarter than they are. R. H. Grant

HAVING A VISION FOR THE INSTITUTION

Leaders without vision are lost from the beginning and can be at best only managers of the events around them. Deans hope that their vision is shared by others, but regardless it is essential that they articulate the vision often and that their decisions be consistent with achieving that vision. For me, the vision was simple and consistent through five administrative posts at four institutions.

First, as administrators in educational institutions, we must create an environment that is conducive to learning, and we must make the learning process enjoyable. We must foster in students the traits of lifelong learning. Even while making learning fun, we must push students to exceed their own expectations of themselves.

Second, specialization and multi-specialty centers or institutes will produce the best research and patient care. With the explosion of knowledge in science and humanities, specialization is necessary not only to continue the advancement of the discipline but also to provide the best-quality patient care. Specialization can best be achieved in a multi-specialty patient care environment (although the patient must have an identifiable person to coordinate that care). I believe that researchers are likely to be more productive in centers or institutes than when isolated by rigid departmental structures.

Third, a quality physical environment is critical for recruiting and retaining the best people. Providing resources for new facilities and providing quality maintenance for salvageable older facilities play a critical role in meeting the tripartite mission of education, research, and patient care.

No matter how busy people are, they are never too busy to stop and tell you how busy they are.

DO WHAT YOU OUGHT TO DO
WHEN YOU OUGHT TO DO IT
WHETHER YOU WANT TO DO IT OR NOT

Everyone recognizes that there is not sufficient time in the day, month, or year to do all of the things one ought to do. How often we hear someone say, "I ought to do this or that but just can't find the time." Yet there are some "oughts" that take precedence over others. The most important of these is the ought of *being available.* If you believe that you are being efficient by tightly screening phone calls and bunching calls to return when it is most convenient for you, you should not be a dean. (This statement also applies to other key administrative positions.) Often, the message you give is to refer the caller to another person in your organization who has delegated authority over that particular activity or issue, but it is quite different for you to talk to the person and explain this fact than for the person to be referred by a mechanical device or even by a skilled secretary. The more contact you have with your constituents, the more understanding they will have of you, the job, and your vision. That is why "management by walking around" has created such a positive effect in many organizations. Don't confuse communication in structured committee meetings, in auditorium presentations, or in writing with personal contact by phone or by scheduled or unscheduled one-on-one or small-group communication, which has far more impact. However, no one wishes to wait days for a response to a letter or an e-mail message. Unfortunately, there is no substitute for working long hours, as best expressed by Longfellow: "The heights by great men reached and kept were not attained by sudden flight but they, while their companions slept, were toiling upwards in the night." The requirements of time are most applicable to the dean's job.

Not to be forgotten in the list of "oughts" is the care of one's self and one's family. Although these concerns cannot become excuses for ignoring other "oughts," scheduled time with the family must be placed high on the "ought" list.

KEEP SMILING

You are the bell-weather for the institutional psyche. If you appear to be happy, if you convey warmth and a smiling, friendly face, others in the institutions will believe that things may not be as bad as they fear. On the other hand, if you appear gloomy and depressed, even those who believe that everything is excellent and couldn't be better will begin to have concerns. Hence, in the true sense, the smile or the depressed face and body language may be the most infectious agent within the institution. Try to infect the entire institution with warmth, a smile, and an upbeat philosophy.

KNOW YOUR FACTS AND BE HONEST

Institutions (even armies) tend to run on rumor. It is essential that you know the rumors and have the staff capacity to dig out the facts. Honesty is a characteristic most admired by society; therefore, be honest before it becomes critical that you do so. Know your facts and convey them honestly and in a direct but thoughtful manner. Honesty that is degrading to a person does not serve a useful purpose and is best left unsaid. Likewise, how one challenges long-held, cherished beliefs is important. Hence, your efforts at being honest need not be direct challenges to others' cherished beliefs but can move them beyond their ideas of right and wrong as you present the facts and move forward.

LEAD, FOLLOW, OR GET OUT OF THE WAY

The saying "Lead, follow, or get out of the way" is at the heart of the dean's dilemma. Organizations that lack leadership drift without direction. It is far better for a leader to make the wrong decision and move an organization in the wrong direction than to have no decision-making capacity. If one sets sail in the wrong direction, the mistake soon becomes evident, and one can change course. Although precious time has been lost, the right course can be found and progress made. Without leadership, an institution-and indeed society as a whole-is like a rudderless ship, getting nowhere while moving in one circle after another. Leadership must be more than the oft-cited cartoon of the dean stating, "There goes my faculty; I must rush to get ahead of them for I am their leader." Although deans are the leaders, they must recognize and support the leadership of other people. This recognition is particularly important when the dean works for a president or vice president who wishes to express a leadership role and direction. Just as we want people to follow our leadership, we must exhibit the ability to follow and support the leadership expressed by others in authority. Thus, it is important to know when to lead and when to follow, and, when neither seems to be appropriate or doable, to get out of the way.

KNOW WHEN TO LEAVE

No one is indispensable, and each person brings some strengths and some weakness to the role of administrator. Without stability in the leadership positions, the institution and organization can suffer. Therefore, a commitment to serve a faculty and an institution for four to six years would appear to be the minimum to provide stability. On the other hand, institutions have suffered equally from keeping institutional leaders in their position when the strengths they bring are no longer needed or have become a part of the institutional culture and the weaknesses they possess are an impediment to growth and the achievement of further successes. For practical purposes, eight to twelve years should be considered the maximum in one position in the same institution. A few, because of energies, insights, and circumstances, may serve effectively slightly longer. I continue to be impressed with the enthusiasm, growth, and progress that follow change in institutional leadership, even when the former leader was the most distinguished and revered of our academic or business community. A critical part of institutional leadership is knowing when to move on. If, indeed, that leader has picked good people and has properly delegated responsibility and authority, the person leaving will be remembered and respected (and frequently loved far more than when in the position), and the person coming in will find the job easier and even more fun.

I am often asked, "What would you change if you had to do it all over again?" My answer is that I would change only two things. First, I would wish that I had known the things that I know now when I started my administrative career. Second, I would wish that I could roll back the clock so that I could have another thirty or more years to enjoy the role of department chairman, dean, vice president, or chancellor in an American medical center.

Chairs (Deans) that have been in the position for many years need to understand that there is a time to reap and a time to sow. If one leaves too early, he lives to regret it, and if he leaves too late, others live to regret it.

When two people in business always agree, one is unnecessary.

7

> "*In the business world it is dog eat dog while in academia, it is just the reverse.*"
> Henry Kiser

REFLECTIONS
ON MY TENURE AS DEAN

Charles H. Epps, Jr., MD

$\mathcal{W}$hen I was appointed dean, I felt honored and proud, for there was little in my past to prepare me for my new position except a high sense of dedication and love for my alma mater. However, relationships and constituencies were affected immediately more than I believed possible.

• My tenured wife and son, both physicians and members of the faculty, were no longer able to remain on the medical school's payroll because of a nepotism rule.

• Fellow faculty members who had been collegial for years became distant. I recognized that true friends remained true, realizing that my official duties and friendship were separate functions.

• Students and staff who related to me in one manner when I was a faculty member now reacted differently. I found that I was perceived to occupy a position of power with significant resources and influence far beyond my true ability and status.

• Learning to say no in different ways without offending and at the same time trying to stave off disappointment became an art form.

• The greatest difference was the uncomfortable fact that my success as dean depended on what I could get others to do, whereas as a surgeon, my success depended largely on my personal cognitive and technical skills.

BAPTISM BY FIRE

As a successful orthopaedic surgeon dealing with emergencies that often threatened life and limb, l had become accustomed to a rapid decision-making process and expedited solutions to solve problems. My patients by and large were grateful for my services, and I received great personal satisfaction at the end of each day because I could count the tasks that I had completed. Nurses, technicians, and other staff, all members of the team, responded promptly to my requests, and the job was done. It was possible for my practice partners and me to hire and fire in a short time frame, pay bills on the spot, and purchase any item according to our preferences. The transition to academic bureaucracy with its inherent inertia and red tape was abrupt and somewhat traumatic.

Having to preside over important changes in the faculty practice plan was my first baptism by fire. Nothing created a deeper chasm between the dean's office and the practicing faculty members than did these money issues. Changing faculty members from independent contractor status to a strict university-based practice plan was disruptive to income flow and long-established practice patterns for senior faculty members. I suspect that some have never forgiven me, although I was carrying out university policy.

The basic science faculty members placed a high value on laboratory space, office space, and even the location of parking spaces. Any change became the source of considerable consternation.

The issues surrounding promotion and the granting of tenure held great importance for both basic science and clinical faculty members. There was a price to pay whenever the will of the departmental or college-wide committees was overturned.

Budget reductions were painful for administrators, faculty members, and staff: we suffered collectively.

ACADEMIC FRUSTRATIONS

The college atmosphere is supposed to be collegial. However, I somehow managed to have law suits filed against me by a student, a staff member, and a faculty member during my term. Even when you prevail, the legal process exacts an emotional toll. I would describe some faculty members as "academic terrorists." It seems that their daily mission was to actively work against and to frustrate the programs of the dean and the university administration. The faculty members were at best mischievous in repeatedly electing these people to positions on crucial committees, such as the grievance committee. However, the presence of these people was balanced by the presence of other hard-working faculty members who were effective teachers, who wrote research grants, and who supported the college and its programs.

DEPARTMENT CHAIRS

Department chairs are the people who actually wield the power, and effective chairs are a joy, making a dean's life easier. However, a few chairs, whom I shall call the "four- thirty bunch," make a habit of dropping by the dean's office at about 4:30 p.m. to unload and to delegate up the ladder the challenging problems that they cannot solve. Unburdened, they go home and leave the dean with additional problems on a plate that is already overflowing. Fortunately, the activities of the four-thirty bunch are balanced by those of dedicated, effective chairmen who run a tight ship.

MEDICAL STUDENTS

Medical students for the most part appreciate the opportunity to study medicine and at the same time generally feel overwhelmed by the volume of material. They are generally nonpolitical, but occasionally the student leadership can become activist. If the activism is constructive, the student-administration relationship is beneficial to both. However, if the leadership is anti- administration, life can be difficult. The fact that the problem students are normally gone in four years at the longest means that time can cure the problem. Perhaps the most emotionally wrenching and painful encounters are those with students who have failed and must be dropped from the college. Bringing in their parents, grandparents, alumni, friends, and ministers only adds to the emotionally charged atmosphere as they plead for readmission. Sometimes it has been possible to persuade students who failed that they should pursue other health care careers, with good results.

UNIVERSITY ADMINISTRATION

The relationship with the central university administration is one that is largely dictated by the budget. I always believed that the college of medicine was and is the crown jewel in our university.

However, the college took its lumps during university-wide reductions and restructuring exercises.

To err is human; to forgive is not university policy.

ALUMNI

Alumni are the first line of support, both financially and politically, for any college. Relationships with the alumni can be strained, particularly when the alumni association is a separately incorporated organization. Confusion reigns in such an arrangement when alumni donate to the alumni association while under the impression that they are contributing directly to the medical school. Occasionally, relationships become strained when alumni demand that their offspring be admitted in spite of poor preparation that makes them noncompetitive, with a premedical record that predicts failure. These situations can be tough and even unpleasant.

ACCREDITATION

Preparing for the necessary accreditation visits of the LCME can be challenging. It is fortunate that the normal cycle is every seven years so that a dean is not likely to have to go through more than one visit, given that the current half-life of a dean is just over three years. Because the threat of loss of accreditation has such dire consequences for any medical school, the stakes are high. Moreover, the dean, who is viewed as responsible (and in fact *is* responsible), has to depend upon the faculty members, staff, and students-in fact, on the entire school community-to be successful. An accreditation visit can be a unifying experience, and success is enjoyed by all. Failure, of course, will most surely rest on the head and shoulders of the dean. Almost as serious for the dean (but more serious for the chairs and program directors) are the periodic accreditation visits by representatives of the Residency Review Committee. I always felt a keen sense of responsibility for these visits. Fortunately, the chairs and program directors have a great deal at stake personally and professionally and work very hard to be successful. There is plenty of happiness and credit to go around when residency programs are successful.

GRADUATION

One day annually during the academic year stands out in my memory as the happiest for me as dean. Our Honors and Oath Day (the day before commencement) is the occasion when the future graduates, in academic regalia, march into the auditorium with faculty members, families, and friends assembled. Departmental prizes for academic achievement are awarded. An alumnus from the twenty-year anniversary class gives the keynote address, and the graduating class recites an updated version of the Hippocratic Oath. Members of the class march across the stage as their names are called to receive scrolls on which the Oath is engraved. One personal innovation that I especially enjoyed was the arrangement for the scroll to be given personally to the graduating senior by a parent or relative who was also an alumnus or by a medical school faculty member. Individual photographs are made to commemorate the occasion.

The turnover of medical school deans in recent years has been rapid and has established the half-life of a dean's tenure at approximately three years. My term as dean allowed me to see six classes graduate before I became Vice President for Health Affairs. During most of my service as dean I also served as Acting Executive Director and CEO of Howard University Hospital. In this manner I came to serve in the four administrative leadership positions of the modern medical center, which have been described by Petersdorf and Wilson as the "four horsemen of the apocalypse."

When I retired from the administration, I experienced mixed emotions. There were accomplishments that gave me a sense of pride and satisfaction. The unpleasant memories have faded with time. On the other hand, pleasant memories remain vivid: the joy of welcoming six freshman classes; the greater joy of seeing 482 seniors graduate with parents and family members showing unbridled happiness and pride; the excitement of a faculty member on receiving a R01 grant; the installation of endowed chairs; the inauguration of endowed lectureships; the notice of approval from the LCME; the receipt of a million-dollar gift; celebrating the 125th anniversary of the founding of the college with a special program featuring Carl Rowan and a gala with Phylicia Rashad and Bill Cosby providing the entertainment. These memories have been made richer and indelible by the realization that these years were a special period in my life but also a special period in the collective lives of the students, staff, faculty members, and administration.

A dean's life is short. Therefore, eat the dessert first.

Sometimes you can't read the handwriting on the wall because the bastards have your back to it.

8

> *"You can only ride a wave if you get ahead of it."*

WHAT'S THIS DEANING
ALL ABOUT, ANYWAY?

C. McCollister Evarts, MD

$\mathcal{T}$he question, "Why become a dean?" has been asked of me on numerous occasions. I suppose that almost everyone in academic life has probably given some thought to one of two polar opposites: becoming a dean or eliminating the dean. This thought is often born out of a desire to retaliate against the exercise of arbitrary authority. So, when asked again about becoming a dean, it seemed time to draw up-short of madness-and reflect upon the reasons.

PERCEIVED OPPORTUNITY-RISKS

One reason for such "madness" was the perceived opportunity to influence the organization at a different level. Certainly, although stress levels are, indeed, high and there are many frustrating circumstances, one does not experience the frustration associated with an inability to create change. It is easier to deal with problems when one can directly influence the outcome.

There is the opportunity to acquire a unique view of an institution, to interface with a wide range of people with greatly varying interests and expertise. Perhaps it is possible to translate one's own ideas into action.

There are distinct risks associated with such a move. A dean's half-life is slightly more than three years. About 25% to 30% of new deans are appointed annually. Being a dean is a gamble at best in today's health care environment.

The academic pathway often leads one to consider deaning. Tracing the evolution from faculty member to chair reveals that at every step one is encouraged to think in broader terms and in regard to institutional issues.

Some semblance of management skills in previous life would appear to contribute to some success as a dean.

Before becoming a dean, it is important - more than that, critical - to make certain that institutional resources be provided for development. Without such guarantees, no one can perform the tasks of deaning.

Perhaps the key to the reasons for becoming a dean lies in the message from a "Hagar the Horrible" cartoon: "If I were content with what I got, I wouldn't be a Viking."

RELATIONSHIPS

What Does a Chair Expect of a Dean?

An informal poll of key chairs revealed certain common qualities expected of a dean. These qualities are generic and equally applicable to a departmental chair and a faculty member:

> *Leadership*, locally, within the university as a whole, and nationally in health-related academic affairs, emphasis on academic excellence and renown first and foremost;
> *Patience*, to which I would add "amen," the impatience of the action-oriented sometimes getting in the way of the necessity for hearing all sides and all parties, and for gathering all available data;
> *A Global View*, of course, without which a dean couldn't function for a moment, with too many secular forces pulling in all directions;
> *Common Sense and Good Judgment*, which go hand in hand;
> *The Ability to Make Decisions*, including difficult ones, an important quality;
> *Recruitment of Talented Chairs*, and then the confidence to allow them to develop clinical teaching and research excellence.

The chairs seem to want a dean who is honest, fair, and compassionate, who has a feel for public relations and some charisma, and who possesses a sense of humor.

The items not listed are the ability to walk on water, speak with God, mint money, and create space!

What Does a Dean Expect of a Chair?

First and foremost, a chair is expected to recruit outstanding faculty members and to provide an environment within that department for the development of the faculty members. This development, of course, provides for the ultimate growth of the institution and the eventual success of a department.

Second, a chair is expected to be committed to the institution, to take a broader view of problems, and to be loyal to the goals of the institution and to those of the individual department. This commitment requires growth on the part of most chairs. When first appointed, chairs make an initial thrust to correct the weakness that have been inherited. The chair's position and that of the department in respect to other departments in the institution need consolidation. However, the dean fervently hopes that, with time, the chair will move toward identifying the problems facing the institution, solving these problems, obtaining resources, developing priorities, and implementing policy for the department and the school. Obviously, this movement will require participation on committees, and much time and effort will be spent on behalf of the school. For understaffed departments, this time commitment is difficult, and for those who have numerous outside interests, it is impossible. A dean certainly does not want a department to exist entirely as an autonomous unit. The mission, the purpose, and the directions of the institution need to be articulated by the chair to the faculty members.

Deans and departmental chairs - particularly heads of large, complex departments - have much in common. Both are problem-solvers, counselors, and consultants. Both are planners and strategists. Both must function as conveners and must serve linking roles within the university. In this regard, the chairs have often been underutilized by deans and, conversely, the essential leadership role of the dean has not been fully appreciated by the faculty.

Third, the dean expects the departmental chair to have valuable expertise or excellence in patient care, coupled with a clear understanding of the changes in health care delivery and the need to provide leadership for the faculty members in this arena. Expertise to varying degrees in teaching and research is expected as well.

Fourth, the chair must be able to communicate and to demonstrate skills in interpersonal relationships.

Fifth, chairs need flexibility, the ability to "roll with the punch."

Finally, I would comment that in the midst of the chaos of an academic medical center in today's world, a sense of humor is a saving grace. If chairs take themselves too seriously, all is lost. One needs the ability to laugh at one's self.

Whenever a chair is sick or injured, send the following note, "The faculty passed a resolution wishing you back to good health. The vote was 322 to 320."

THE REALITY INDEX

After the aforementioned construction of the ideal relationships, both from the viewpoint of the chair and from that of the dean, what is a reality index?

First and foremost is the observation that most faculty members lack institutional commitment. As a matter of fact, some of them have a much greater sense of loyalty to a national subspecialty organization than they do to their own institution.

Second, emphasis is placed on *my, mine, ours*, etc., particularly in regard to space. Most are prepared to show the folly of the concept of university space. Who among us has not said, with a ringing tone of authority, "This is my space." ? Interference of any kind leads to the declaration, "By God, you will not trample on my rights any further."

Dean-bashing is a favorite pastime. Some of that is obviously to be expected, but often it is not particularly productive. After all, who else would be foolish enough to take the job? Consider the alternatives!

One of the primary problems facing academic medical centers is the inability of faculty members to maintain confidentiality. For some reason, leaks are prevalent; they in turn lead to rumors, adding to the general unrest of the institution.

*F*amous faculty quote:
        My fellows, our residents, the students

THE FITNESS TRAIL OF DEANING

There are certain stations along the trail of deaning that contribute to the fitness of any deanship. Let me mention a few.

The first is to *prepare for the unexpected*, because you can be certain that the unexpected will, indeed, happen. One should try to never be surprised. This, of course, means developing a good network of communication and setting the time to reflect upon what might be the ramifications of an action or a situation.

The second stop along the fitness trail is to *be aware of the constituencies served*. There are staggering numbers of constituencies: the faculty members; the chairs; the staff; the community; the accreditation bodies; the patients; the unions; the students; the federal, state, and local governments; special societies and boards; the alumni; the university president; and the board of trustees, to name a few. All of these constituencies affect the dean. All of the constituent groups measure the dean by different standards. One must develop priorities among the constituencies, trying for good relationships with each. However, it must be recognized from the outset that it will be impossible to serve all constituencies with equal vigor and no two constituencies will rate your performance the same.

The next step is *the ability to delegate*. This ability must be carefully activated. It is essential to the functioning of an academic medical center.

The next stop along the fitness trail is to recall Henry Rosovsky's admonition, "Never underestimate the difficulty of changing false beliefs by facts." The rumor mill, a flourishing enterprise of the academic medical center, produces rumors that soon become fact.

It is then extremely difficult to convince anyone that the rumor is not true, even though the facts point to the contrary.

Moving up the hill, there is the need to educate the faculty and others about the meaning of the word "*responsive.*" Responsive means saying yes, but it also means saying no. Most interpret responsiveness as saying yes. It is quite clear that one must say no more than yes. As a matter of fact, one famous president was asked what he did most often, and that was, he said no.

A dean needs to *avoid a sense of impatience*, especially when dealing with the inertia of a large institution. It is clear that almost anything takes some time to accomplish, and large events take longer. Under these circumstances, patience is a virtue. *Keep quiet and listen!* There is always the inclination to talk too much. This is dangerous, because almost every word is given added meaning with interpretation ranging over 360 degrees. The dean needs to be able to convince others to give something to the institution, to get something for the institution, or to get out of the institution. This should be applied to all of the staff and administrative personnel as well as to the faculty members. Unfortunately, academic medical centers protect the incompetent.

As important as any station along the fitness trail of deaning is to *avoid the urgent overcoming the important.* Everything is urgent-all calls are urgent, all meetings are urgent, everyone urgently has to see the dean. However, not all are equally important. The personal calendar becomes all important.

Finally, it is absolutely essential that the dean *retain a sense of humor.* If you have never had a sense of humor, I suspect you are already hopelessly lost!

I was recruiting a chair recently and as we were walking into the medical center, she asked, "How many people work here?" I had to say, "About half."

ANECDOTES

Is life bearable as a dean, or is the deanship one endless struggle of budgets, space, complaints, faculty unrest, student demonstrations, employee discontent, trustee demands, presidential expectations, and the like?

Several things come to mind. All centers have a life of their own, yet there seem to be certain generic, inalienable rights. These would include parking, smoking, and space.

My first encounter with parking was to arrive from an academic medical center with limited parking and paid parking to a center of 550 acres. Free parking was a privilege that had subsequently evolved to become an inalienable right. Looking at the budget and deciding that a source of funding for the library could be paid parking, I thought the logic seemed perfect. However, several petitions later, amid threats of mass resignation and patient flight, the decision was deferred. It took two years to accomplish paid parking. (No one resigned; our clinic population has grown each year.)

Trying to benefit somewhat from this experience, I approached the smoking policy in a different manner. After deciding that the institution would become a "No Smoking" institution, I prepared guidelines with large amounts of data supporting the horrors of smoking. An edict of no smoking was finally announced to the institution in a manner that some considered clever and shrewd and others considered to be pure and unadulterated cowardice. The day after the announcement, I left on vacation!

Space, of course, is the third inalienable right. It didn't take long after my arrival at Penn State's Hershey Medical Center for me to recognize that there was no space for development of new programs or even the sustenance of old programs. From the outset of the school, there had been a considerable amount of space set aside for student cubicles for study purposes. However, with a decreasing class size, there were extra cubicles, and again it seemed quite logical to use part of the cubicle space for an expansion to allow the recruitment of a new Chair of Medicine. This decision was greeted by a massive uprising of the student body and letters to the Board of Trustees, the President of the University, and anyone else who could read. However, the space was given to Medicine, and we were successful in recruiting an excellent new Chair of Medicine. The students did not let this go unnoticed, and in a small display case of the institution showing buildings of the campus, they placed a series of dinosaurs around the location of the administrative offices. These dinosaurs were ringed by armed troops firing upon the dinosaurs. The message seemed crystal clear-the dinosaurs of the administration should be eliminated!

Another episode (for me, unique) focused on a call from a federal bureaucrat who informed me that the institution was in serious violation of a well-established regulation. I inquired exactly what this regulation was after the caller said that our federal funding might be withdrawn. He informed me that one could not use the myoglobin from sperm whales for research. This research, of course, was a bit distant from the orthopaedist's daily routine. I said that I really wasn't aware that we were using much of this myoglobin, but that I would investigate it further. The upshot was that five or six years earlier someone had obtained some myoglobin from a sperm whale for some research but was not using it and had no plans for using it in the future. Another phone call to the bureaucrat reassured him that we were, indeed, legitimate in our nonusage of myoglobin from the sperm whale, and we promised never to even think of this again. He withdrew his threat, and I hope he is whistling happily forever after in the bowels of some Washington office.

Another interesting matter involved the move of one of our recruits. Recognizing that one must be sensitive to the animal activists in this day and age, I was somewhat unprepared for a bill that arrived for $396.86, in addition to the moving expenses of this particular faculty member. It turned out that the bill was documented by a form from the "Pussy Paws Motel, Inc."-an exclusive vacation home for your "pampered" cat. The bill was submitted by this faculty member for cat care for a period of 23 days. This, according to my Executive Assistant, was the first time such a bill had been submitted in the school's history.

I suppose to best illustrate the wide variation of daily events, I would cite the following personal experience: the day had extended somewhat longer than usual, and I found myself on the ward visiting one of my patients at about 10:00 p.m. I entered the patient's room to find a nurse and a medical student-a strapping young man-struggling with the patient's intravenous line. They turned to me as what seemed to be a source of help. Not knowing quite what to do, I acted as though I had been starting IVs for a long time, and by a combination of blind luck and some quick moves, the IV began to run again.

We left the room with the following thoughts running through my mind: What a wonderful example I was to this young medical student. Here was the dean, late at night, visiting his patient, serving as a role model, starting an intravenous line - this is great! I sort of stepped back as the student came up to me, expecting him to make some reference to this series of events. He looked me in the eye and asked, "You are the Dean?" I responded, "Yes." "I have a question for you." Expecting that he was going to ask something about patient care under these exemplary circumstances, I nodded. He then asked, "Why is the helicopter landing on our rugby field?"

> *A dean must have a sense of humor and a lack of sense to survive.*

CONCLUSIONS - CIRCA 1997

After a decade in the position, I find that a few things seem obvious:

• less strength of the deanship in academic medicine (Many qualified individuals will not consider this type of leadership. There are many more constraints - "More barbed wire around small corrals.");

• more federal and state control;

• more participation by lawyers in academic policy;

• more influence by faculty members on appointments and promotion;

• more demands by faculty members in regard to governance and academic policy;

• more objectives to be met and more ambiguity of goals;

• rapidly escalating fiscal constraints with decreasing sources of funding to support the academic mission;

• less chance for institutions to grow and to make changes in the process of growth;

• less respect of science and medicine by the general public;

• a demand for "accountability" and for change by the general public; and

• the profound impact of managed care upon academic health centers.

One must accept these constraints as a given and try to move forward toward leading a dynamic readjustment of the academic health center. Opportunities in the evolving health care world of managed care must be identified. Change is essential for survival. The academic mission must be preserved.

To meet these challenges, a changing pattern of transforming leadership must emerge-leadership that creates institutional purpose; leadership that is concerned with broad issues and with the minutiae; leadership that allows institutional members to transcend daily affairs.

Transforming leadership occurs in such a way that leaders and followers raise one another to higher levels of motivation and morality. Purposes that might have started out as separate but related become fused. Power bases are linked, not as counter weights but as mutual support for common purpose. It is a dynamic leadership in the sense that the leaders create a relationship with followers who will feel elevated by it and often become more active themselves, thereby creating new cadre of leaders.

I hope the deans (leaders) of tomorrow will be different from some of the leaders of the past. They will not lead by fear, domination, or seduction. Their faults will be apparent. They will demonstrate that institutional university bureaucracy can be revitalized and consensus developed.

James MacGregor Burns contends that we must move from positions of transactional leadership - bargaining, trading, transacting - toward leadership that demonstrates genuine moral values, common aspirations, and goals, toward a transforming leadership in which leaders see and act on their own values and motivations and those of their followers.

One thing is clear: academic health centers must have deans who are transforming leaders. It makes a great difference who they are.

Finally, one of the most urgent concerns for academic medicine is the survival of the academic mission - teaching, research, and patient care. This, in part, is what deaning is all about.

Medical schools are about the future. We teach not only current information but the future of health care and we conduct the research that leads to tomorrow's medicine. When discussing the future, statements from these philosophers may be helpful:

"We stand at a crossroads. One leads to hopelessness and the other to utter despair. We must have the courage to make the right decision." Woody Allen

"I can predict anything but the future." Woody Allen

"All of your future is ahead of you." Curt Gowdy

"If you come to a fork in the road, take it." Yogi Berra

9

An academic health center is defined as 1000 points of veto.

LEADERSHIP ROLES IN THE ACADEMIC MEDICAL CENTER

Christopher C. Fordham, III, MD

$\mathcal{A}$t the 125 medical schools in the United States, the responsibilities of the dean and the medical faculty vary tremendously. It is generally agreed that the academic medical center is one of the more complex organizations in modern society and that the medical school deanship and other executive posts are extraordinarily difficult positions to hold. Somber publications and public discussions about the deanship, by experienced and knowledgeable people,[1] have stressed the negative aspects of the position and the severity of its problems.

Although medical schools and their faculties and deans exist within highly fluid academic and management structures, I firmly believe that another point of view is warranted. It is my opinion that the deanship is an exciting leadership post, replete with opportunities for constructive and challenging self expression, and offering potential satisfactions that far outweigh the acknowledged frustrations. The positions of dean, department head, or division chief in academic medical centers certainly do not appeal to the timid or the "laid back;" these positions require a demanding, even consuming, way of life. But they also offer choice opportunities for growth within a framework of challenge and high adventure that will surely continue to attract candidates who possess strong human and leadership qualities.

PROBLEMS AND OPPORTUNITIES

Structural Relationships

The problems I have encountered at my own institution and have seen at other institutions relate to the structural relationships of various administrators within the academic medical center and particularly to the dean's role vis-a-vis a vice president or vice chancellor and hospital CEO. This relationship is particularly problematic in consideration of the management responsibility assigned to each role and the authority granted to carry out these responsibilities. Further complications may arise as the leader of the academic unit becomes part of a major university with yet another layer of administrators. The problems associated with the capacity to provide faculty leadership and to make and carry out appropriate decisions may be lessened when one person serves as both vice president and dean, but combining the roles does not eliminate the need for a precise delineation of functions and responsibilities at the several levels of administrative hierarchy in academic medical centers and the universities to which they belong.

Deans face problems and opportunities within the framework of institutions at which they and the faculty members carry a large portion of the responsibility for the academic medical center: namely, the assignment of space and budget, critical involvement in the appointment of the hospital director, and management capabilities characterized by a strongly organized dean's office, including planning and fiscal activities. If in fact those who hold these responsibilities respond to other offices, then in effect the dean becomes an academic affairs officer, regardless of formal title. It may not matter what title the chief executive officer of the academic medical center holds, whether chancellor, president, vice president, or dean, but it does matter that the faculty members and administrative officers understand the arrangement and clearly comprehend functions and accountability. Conflicts commonly arise from ambiguities related to these roles.

Regardless of the organization of the academic medical center (defined as the principal teaching hospital and medical school), critical responsibility for the conduct of affairs should lie upon the shoulders of the faculty members of the school of medicine and its leadership. In my view, it is vital that the dean adopt the role of "dean of the faculty," particularly because that body reflects the various expectations and requirements of the school's constituencies. The dean represents the faculty members in fostering the support and understanding of those constituencies and in promoting the best interests of the institution and those it serves. The faculty members must fully trust the dean and know that their objectives will be merged with those of the medical center. If the dean views the faculty members as merely one of the constituencies of the school, the burden of leadership is much more likely to become isolated and thereby constrain the prospects for strong performance.

The leadership and management problems are further compounded by the rising importance of other health professional schools and indeed the interests that some of them have in the teaching hospital. Close collaboration among the schools is imperative, and access to the teaching hospital must be assured for the schools of dentistry, nursing, and pharmacy. I believe that this collaboration and access can best be provided by collegiality among the groups and need not require that an executive officer manage the activities of the health sciences center.

Educating Medical Students

Medical education needs to be better integrated into our university educational system. The magnitude and scope of the academic medical center, which often is nearly equal to those of the rest of the university, set it apart in some ways. First, the commitment to service is ordinarily deeper than in other parts of the university because of the teaching hospital. Second, the faculty-student ratio tends to be among the highest in academia because of a large proportion of one-on-one graduate clinical teaching. Third, the dependence on faculty-generated funding for clinical research and training is greater than in most other parts of the university. Fourth, public visibility is high, and public expectations are sometimes unrealistic. Furthermore, teachers of medicine increasingly need to draw on the knowledge, insights, and approaches of all of the scholarly disciplines and gifted minds in the university. Indeed joint appointments and functions with such disciplines as history, anthropology, economics, law, public policy, philosophy, ethics, and the arts and humanities are important. Conversely, other parts of the university can benefit from the association with medical and biomedical science.

The Teaching Hospital

Whatever the governance structure in a given institution, the teaching hospital is the keystone of an academic medical center. The medical dean, hospital director, and medical faculty - who must be peers and partners in more of a marriage than a dichotomy - bear the main responsibility for the hospital's operation and success. The management problems are formidable, especially in large and complicated tertiary and quaternary facilities. It is therefore quite obvious that the hospital and the patient care facilities represent an integral part of university-based medical education. It is also apparent that the dean and the clinical department heads must make an important commitment to all facets of the hospital's operations. The basic science chairs should also have a stake in this enterprise.

Collegiality

Aside from the impact of the organization of the university and the academic medical center on the role of medical deans, various other factors limit their capacity to exercise authority commensurate with responsibility. These factors include relationships with granting agencies, professional societies, and the teaching hospital; various aspects of the work of the faculty members that divide their loyalties; and the need of the staff professionals and scientists to maintain close liaison with their discipline so that they can maintain their technical identity and advance their professionalism. But the primary restraint on the dean's authority - one that is desirable and necessary - is the collegial nature of the medical dean's leadership role. The legitimacy and power of the position have derived fundamentally from the credibility and trust that the occupant has shared with the faculty members. It is true that the collegial environment may lend itself to discord, posture, and stagnation, but it need not be so. My own experience is that department chairs, division chiefs, hospital directors, and faculty members at large can be stimulated to identify with the institution's needs and responsibilities.

The Dean and Department Chairs as Leaders

The role and the responsibility of the dean in relationships with department chairs are critical. Department chairs must be both managers and scholars. Yet the fact that few scholars are trained as managers presents a dilemma to search committees, institutions, and the entire academic community. Because department chairs are key institutional leaders in a medical school, they must cultivate the capacity to wear both departmental and institutional hats. This duality of roles presents a special challenge because of competition for limited resources and pressures from faculty colleagues. Thus, at various times and to varying degrees, the medical school dean and other key center personnel must be leaders, administrators, managers, planners, strategists, coordinators, counselors, communicators, consultants, educators, public relations-financial-personnel officers, bureaucrats, negotiators, fund raisers - and sometimes even visionaries and prophets. Certain personality traits and characteristics are sought in all executives: personableness, intelligence, integrity, decisiveness, a sense of responsibility, good judgment, credibility, initiative, impartiality, enthusiasm, physical and emotional health and stamina, resilience, perseverance, patience, and, perhaps most importantly, equanimity, as well as serenity of spirit. In addition, most leaders should be able to speak well publicly; to identify and focus on the right problem; to devise the best approach for solving problems and to assign the appropriate individuals or groups to the effort; to stimulate people to cooperate in the attainment of common objectives; to endure criticism and live with uncertainties; to establish agendas; to designate priorities; to sense political nuances, both internal and external; and to derive satisfaction and challenge from productive interpersonal relationships.

Necessary Attributes

Although all of these attributes are desirable and are probably only rarely found in one person, certain attributes stand out as necessary for a successful and enjoyable deanship.

Probably the most important attribute is the desire to serve others. I would guess that about 90% of the dean's time is spent in serving others - supporting and facilitating the work of faculty members, staff, and students. Deans cannot boss or be the boss of these groups. Although the position of dean or some other academic administrator may sound prestigious, status and a sense of power or authority, as self-aggrandizing as they may be, have resulted in the downfall of many deans and other academic administrators.

The second most important attribute is academic statesmanship. Although this attribute is easy to define in broad, general terms, analyzing its essential ingredients is far more difficult and is subject to personal bias. I believe that statesmanship embraces the ability or capacity to mobilize and sustain the support and trust of key constituencies; to place the institution ahead of self and self-aggrandizement; to maintain continual vigilance about the best interests of the organization; to balance short-term and limited self-interest with the long-term interests of the constituencies and society at large; and to help move the organization forward within the proceeding framework.

Deans must possess the capacity to conceptualize complicated issues and problems, to ask the right questions, and to formulate rational approaches. It is also extremely helpful if they can articulate their views on these matters succinctly and with clarity.

Deans and other academic administrators must be willing to listen to the views of others. Even after spending years in administrative positions, deans face the ever-present risk of adopting "reflex" responses. Yet each questioner's problem is meaningful to the person who presents it and deserves a thoughtful, reassuring answer. On the other hand, reflex answers often create distress and distrust.

Deans must possess the capacity to delegate. A key ingredient of leadership is the capacity to delegate duties, responsibilities, and authority. One person in a complex organizational hierarchy cannot pay adequate attention to all matters that deserve attention. Thus, delegation helps get things done properly. Beyond that, delegation not only builds confidence and trust in associates but also enables them to enjoy professional satisfaction.

Deans must foster constituency support. Communication skills sharpen the overall proficiency of medical executives, especially deans. Deans must communicate smoothly with the academic medical center, its leaders, faculty members, and students; with university officials; with community, state, regional, and national leaders and dignitaries; with alumni; with professional associates; and with the general public. Smooth communication requires an excellent grasp of educational, socioeconomic, and political factors at all levels. Knowledge that the dean is accessible is reassuring to faculty members, staff, and students. Impromptu visits to department heads without an agenda can be valuable and time saving. It is important to schedule appointments with the department heads in their offices: such an action sends a good message and at the same time gives more flexibility with respect to timing the visit. Much can be accomplished by responding even to calls that promise to be unpleasant: prompt and emphatic reactions can often defuse possible crises. The degree to which one can thank, cajole, motivate, and learn from thoughtful use of the telephone is rarely appreciated.

SPECIAL CHALLENGES AND PROBLEMS

A special problem that affects the dean more than any other academic administrator is the wide variety of challenges and problems faced in recruiting and managing executive personnel. Few executives have more than eight or ten people reporting directly to them; deans, on the other hand, have all department chairs, center directors, and a variety of other individuals directly responsible to them.

The selection and recruitment of departmental chairs is the area in which the dean can have the most lasting institutional impact. Appointing an excellent search committee is not in itself sufficient. It is essential that the members of the search committee know the type of candidate sought, the current assets and weaknesses of the unit, and the resources that are available. Certain ground rules should be in place from the onset: e.g., no appointment to a post will be offered to people who are not among those recommended by the committee as long as it is constituted; in turn, the dean bears no obligation to appoint any nominees unless one of them is found acceptable. After candidates have been formally recommended by the committee, it becomes the dean's responsibility to consummate the process through negotiation and recruitment. In my experience, it is frequently desirable for the chair of the search committee and perhaps the dean to conduct initial interviews with candidates selected by the committee at sites away from the school. These candidates should not ordinarily be permitted to visit the campus unless paperwork, personal references, and telephone conversations suggest significant potential for an appointment. An essential aspect of the recruitment process is a vigorous affirmative action program. Affirmative action is often misunderstood. What it really means is an inclusionary search. Such a search will inevitably result in an increasing number of new appointments from traditionally underrepresented groups, thereby enriching the diversity and often the quality of the institution.

In addition to the recruitment and appointment process is that of the assessment of performance. All administrators should undergo periodic reviews (usually at five-year intervals). The reviews should not occupy the time and energy of a faculty-wide committee; instead, a small committee of carefully selected people should be charged to carry out a simple and brief review that avoids lengthy and needless wheel spinning. In units where things are clearly not going well, conversations with the person to be reviewed should precede the appointment of the review committee so that the incumbent will be given the opportunity to take the initiative in making a change. Sometimes the dean will need to give careful and gracious guidance in this process. Such a process can provide the key opportunity for the gracious exit of a valued or even distinguished colleague who is now ineffective in an administrative post.

It is also important not to overlook the unique role of the dean's office staff. By their attitudes, these office personnel set, to a significant degree, the tone of a friendly, responsive, and competent organization. The foremost requirement for a staff is a first-class chief secretary or administrative assistant. This person should be able to manage the office astutely, communicate openly and candidly with the chief, and maintain the fine line between appropriate accessibility and reasonable protection.

REWARDS AND SATISFACTIONS

Especially because of the inherent restrictions on their authority and their basic role as coordinator rather than as direct managers, executives in an academic medical center - especially deans - must be able to derive satisfaction and pride from the achievements of their institutions, departments, and personnel. These rewards, which sometimes bring unmitigated joy, lighten the undeniably heavy burdens of the office. Recognition of one's own effort is of course always satisfying, but the achievements of others are the most heartwarming. What greater solace can there be than knowing that one has fostered the environment that makes it possible for other people to grow personally and professionally?

Equally important to one's own satisfaction is the crucial issue of recognizing when one is at the end of the road. It is incumbent upon the dean to bear the burden of sensing when a change will best serve the institution and to formulate plans for a smooth transition. Warning signs are clear: fatigue sets in. The "issue carousel" tends repeatedly to bring around issues that grow tiresome. One can not enthusiastically attack old and new problems. It is highly beneficial to the institution if this battle fatigue does not occur too soon, because change of leadership is disruptive to any organization. In my judgment, the optimal range of effective service for most deans, department heads, and division chiefs is between five and ten years. Some administrators know after only a few months in the job that their tenure will not be long, and their colleagues will probably have reached the same conclusion. In those instances, a tour of duty of two to four years is usual. A few relatively rare people may serve somewhat beyond ten years. All too often, a new executive officer arrives on the scene weeks to months after the predecessor's departure. This type of transition can be so disruptive to the institution, and indeed at times the problems facing the new person are so urgent, that some deans may fail because a disruptive transition places an intolerable burden on the incoming dean. This burden leads to an early weakening in the confidence of the faculty and other constituents as well as the incumbent. Therefore, in my opinion the institution will best be served if the outgoing dean, when possible, stays at the post and tries to move things forward until the very day on which the successor arrives. The fullest possible briefing should then be followed by a prompt and gracious exit.

It should be evident that this essayist believes that collegiality, perseverance, and joy in the achievements of others go miles and miles toward creating extraordinary personal satisfaction through professional work. When faculties are strong in spirit and their leadership at several levels matches these qualities, what they can achieve with reasonable resources is truly remarkable. The joy of leadership is having a hand in facilitating such achievement on behalf of institutional service and the advancement of society.

Reference

1   Robert J. Glaser, "The Medical Deanship: Its Half Life and Hard Times" *Journal of Medical Education* 44 December, 1969; David E. Rogers, "Reflections on a Medical School Deanship" The Faros of Alpha Omega Alpha 38 No. 3, July 1975; Ralph W. Ingersoll, "The Deanly Condition" *Journal of Medical Education* 50 October, 1975.

This is a story about four people named everybody, somebody, anybody and nobody. There was an important job to be done and everybody was asked to do it. Everybody was sure somebody would do it, anybody could have done it, but nobody did it. Somebody got angry about that because it was everybody's job. Everybody thought anybody could do it, but nobody realized that everybody wouldn't do it. It ended up that everybody blamed somebody when nobody did what anybody could have done.

10

> T*hings may come to those who wait*
> *but only the things left by those who hustle."*
>
> Abraham Lincoln

AN
ADMINISTRATIVE
PERSPECTIVE

James F. Glenn, MD

*I*t can be categorically stated that no one is ever fully prepared to assume a major medical administrative role - dean, hospital director, medical center president. No matter what previous experience has been gained in supportive roles, the blunt impact of making necessary decisions will come with shocking force upon the neophyte administrator. I can certify that the result is significant.

NEGATIVE IMAGES OF A DEANSHIP

Literally within hours of the time that I indicated my intention to become a dean, my friends and colleagues began to inundate me with bad jokes, many of them familiar to other deans. Most deans and former deans will have heard that "old deans never die; they just lose their faculties." Or the ever popular analogy, "Deans are like mushrooms: they are kept in the dark, nurtured on horse manure, and after a year or so, they are canned." There are countless other quasi-clever commentaries, but many of them are too lewd for publication.

There are many routes to the dean's office. Most commonly, a person who has demonstrated competence as a department chair is tapped for the opportunity to become a dean. Success as a chair, however, does not guarantee success as a dean, because the variables are infinitely greater.

All too often, incompetence may be rewarded as well. Dr. Smith, a faculty member, has a lagging clinical practice or loses grant support, but tenure demands that he be retained on the faculty. As a consequence, the failing faculty member may be invited to join the dean's staff as an assistant or associate dean for one or another activities of the medical school, such as research, clinical practice, admissions, curriculum, and so forth. Then one day the dean abruptly expires or is lured away to another opportunity. The search committee makes a desultory effort to identify a replacement, finally deciding that old Smith, the associate dean, already has a key to the washroom and has been around long enough to have some vague idea of what is going on in the dean's office. The failure continues to fail.

> *If we aren't careful, we are likely to go in the direction in which we are going.* Yogi Berra

DEALING WITH LAY BOARDS

Of course, a dean or any other medical administrator does not function in a vacuum. There is always some authority to which that administrator must report. Frequently the dean is responsible to a vice president of the university, the president himself, or a chancellor for medical affairs. Usually these people are fairly conversant with the mission and are therefore supportive. On the other hand, the worst nightmare will be realized when the dean must report to a board of directors or trustees, composed primarily of lay people. This is a virtually impossible situation, because the lay people selected for such board service are often very successful in their own right and, consequently, are very opinionated about how a medical school, hospital, or medical center should be run. The medical administrator is forever defending one rational position after another against irrational criticism.

Planning for a new hospital at Mt. Sinai Medical Center had been in progress for some eight years at the time of my arrival. The concept at that point was to build a high-rise tower on Madison Avenue overlooking East Harlem. I saw this concept as a disaster; therefore, I approached the trustees with the idea of a low-rise building focused on Central Park. This vision required the demolition of some 23 old and antiquated buildings that had some sentimental value but little else to offer. After several frustrating and unproductive meetings, we still had not reached closure on the issue. Finally, in exasperation, I said, "A vertical hospital doesn't work; a horizontal hospital does." Fortunately, one of the trustees rose to the occasion as the perfect straight man, asking, "Why is that, doctor?" I replied, "Because you can push a stretcher horizontally, but not vertically." The matter was resolved, and with the help of the wonderful I. M. Pei, we designed and built a beautiful new low-rise facility.

DEANS AS LISTENERS

The best deans are undoubtedly those who are the best listeners, preferably with infinite patience. Perhaps this accounts for the fact that so many deans are psychiatrists. Alternatively, there are a number of pediatricians who have occupied dean's offices, prompting the comment that this is appropriate because so many faculty members are childish in their expectations and performance.

I have always been interested in primates, but the most fascinating are certainly the great apes weighing 600 pounds and more. One must be cautious in observing these spectacular beasts, because direct eye contact with them will prompt rage. A favorite retaliation of these gorillas is to throw feces through the bars of the cage at the offending visitor. Deans may find a familiar theme here, having dealt with recalcitrant faculty members who react in a similar fashion.

On the other hand, the apes provided inspiration to me. One extensive study revealed that these apes could learn to communicate by sound and sign language. I reasoned that if they were trainable in this fashion, they might be taught to accomplish deanly chores. I realized that I could save a tremendous amount of time if I could teach one of the apes two functions: first, the animal would be taught to answer the telephone, say "Dean Glenn," and then just listen interminably until the caller hung up; second, I would hope that the beast could be taught to sign my name on the endless pieces of paper that came across the desk.

Every day the lion walked through the jungle asking the other animals who was king of the jungle. Everyone he asked said the lion was the king of the jungle until one day the lion asked an elephant. The elephant promptly beat up the lion and the lion said, "Just because you don't know the answer, you don't have to get angry about it."

ORGANIZATIONAL PROBLEMS

One of the most significant problems facing a dean is the structure of academic medical institutions. For a variety of reasons, departments have proliferated over the years, sometimes to the point that the dean must interface and interact directly with as many as fifty or sixty people who are academic or organizational department heads. This interaction becomes an almost impossible chore, and many institutions have sought to simplify matters by developing an executive committee. All too often, this effort is thwarted by internal competition and jealousies. A host of other organizational and structural ideas have been promoted. Most experts feel that an executive can only interface effectively with a handful of administrators. With this appealing idea in mind, one could suggest reconstituting the academic departments into perhaps five sections: a division of basic sciences, women and children's specialties, primary care, medical specialties, and surgical specialties. An alternative approach is the horizontal organization based upon organ system orientation, such as neurosciences, cardiopulmonary diseases, nephrourology, and so on, However, this organizational structure gets a little messy when too many medical and surgical specialties are involved in one organ group.

FINANCIAL ISSUES

No reflections on the challenges to medical administrators would be complete without some commentary on the financial aspects of the medical education enterprise. Education is a costly business, a fact that seems to have escaped the attention of politicians and the general public. All too often, the medical school faculty members are expected to make their own way entirely through the practice of medicine. This expectation immediately fosters a conflict of interests, because generation of income may often take precedence over the teaching responsibilities of a faculty member. Somehow, we must reinforce the need for adequate financial support of the teaching enterprise. Fortunately, enlightened hospital administrators recognize the need for support of various academic endeavors and will often allocate financial resources for support of the teaching effort.

The frustrations in trying to steer the course of a medical school, hospital, and medical center are many and diverse. Perhaps the biggest frustration of all is the fact that the administrator must say no to many good proposals, simply because there are not the resources to support the project.

Would I do it over again? You bet! I do not know of anything more fun that you can do with all of your clothes on.

I was at a faculty meeting the other day and we were having a tremendous argument about space. In fact one faculty member got up and called me a horses rear-end (not necessarily in those terms). When he did, four or five faculty members around him quickly ushered him out of the room. I was impressed by this and turned to the chair of Faculty Council and said, "I didn't realize the faculty liked me that much" to which he answered, "They don't, they like horses."

11

*If you don't have time to do it right,
when will you have time to do it over?*

*No man knows his strengths who
does not know his weakness.*

A NEED FOR STABILITY

James A. Hallock, MD

$\mathcal{A}$fter almost ten years as a dean, I have found it to be a most rewarding, challenging, and stimulating position, while at the same time a most demanding and, at times, frustrating position. My comments for "Reflections" reflect a deep concern about the continuing turnover of the deanship in schools of medicine and the decrease in time of tenure of deans. Whether or not the length of term equates with success, it definitely serves as one measure of success. It seems impossible that there can be any significant stable approach to educational policy on a national and local level if the leadership is in constant turmoil and turnover. My hope is that one outcome of this publication will be an increase in the success and stability of the medical deanships of this country.

WHAT MAKES FOR STABILITY

As I think about the reasons for the length of my tenure, several things come to mind:

• First, the support of the administration of the university. The chancellor who recruited me, and to whom I directly report, has not changed over this period of time. We have developed a mutually supportive relationship that has allowed me to act as, and be perceived as, the leader of the medical school.

• Second, the match between the institution and me, and the fact that each has benefited. This match may be difficult to measure and intangible, but it is important. The expectations that were initially presented to me have remained constant and have evolved in a mutual fashion over the past ten years.

• Third, the environment around us. This environment has not changed as rapidly or drastically as it has in other places. This stability has allowed us a more deliberate approach to change and perhaps less chaos in our system.

• Fourth, risks taken along the way. Some of these risks have paid off and have allowed the school to be recognized in areas of primary care, telemedicine, rural medicine, and now minimally invasive surgical procedures. If we had not taken these risks, the "success" we have enjoyed would not be the same.

NATIONAL RECOGNITION

During my second year as dean, a member of the board of trustees challenged me that one of my roles should be to obtain national recognition for the institution. That goal has been a driving force causing me personally and members of my staff to become involved in national activities that assist in the recognition of the institution. People no longer ask whether East Carolina is a separate state, or which state it happens to be in. At least to this point, we have not created a new state.

THE NEGATIVES

The two most distressing aspects of this position are dealing with personnel matters and effecting cultural change. Personnel matters related to relieving department chairs of their duty and decisions not to confer tenure or promotion are among the very distressing and difficult aspects of the deanship. In addition, the attendant personnel grievance issues and related matters drain energy away from the creative side of the position.

Effecting cultural change in the institution at a time when local external forces are not forcing change is difficult and demands a great deal of effort. It is disappointing to work for months with chairs or selected faculty members on an issue or problem and then to step away and conclude that "they just don't get it." Perhaps that's a personal shortcoming, but it is among the most frustrating portions of the position.

THE DEAN AS LEADER

The dean is clearly the leader of the faculty and needs to set the education, research, and clinical agenda as well as manage a multi-million-dollar corporate enterprise and serve as a negotiator and a fund-raiser. Unfortunately, most deans are best at serving as educational leaders but they rarely put the necessary energy into that portion of the position. We may get great positive feedback from interacting with students; however, we spend too little time with students and their teachers (our faculty members). Corporate management, negotiating, and fundraising, which are vital to the sustenance and maintenance of the institution, demand great time and energy, but often the return on effort is less than could be perceived.

An interesting misunderstanding is the role of the dean in the admission of students to the school of medicine. Most institutions (and in ours in particular) have set policies regarding the characteristics of students to be accepted, but the admissions committee is charged with and left alone to make the decisions as to who is admitted. At least weekly, if not daily, influential people are contacting the dean and attempting to sway the admission of students who they claim will be future primary care leaders, primary care physicians, and rural doctors. Thus far, I have transmitted information to the admissions committee but have not tampered in any way with decisions that are made. About three years ago I received a call from a medical school classmate whom I had not seen in thirty years. He wanted to have his daughter admitted to medical school. When asked whether she was a North Carolina resident, he answered, of course, that she was not; she was a New Jersey resident. I told my friend that I could not help him, and he quickly replied, "You sound like a Southerner." People have the misperception that the dean is perhaps more powerful and influential than is truly the situation.

The overwhelming positives of this position are the ability to influence an educational program and move it forward in line with the mission of the institution; to affect the health care of a region; to provide resources and to see very bright people become very creative and very productive. To accomplish these goals, it is crucial that the dean be perceived as an optimistic leader and as one who appears to under-stand the issues. The dean may not necessarily have a solution to every problem but certainly must be willing to address problems and to lis-ten to and understand situations presented by faculty members and other constituents.

Is this a complex situation? Indeed it is! It would be as com-plex as having to put together a jigsaw puzzle entitled "Medical School" but with no picture on the box. Frequently, a few pieces fall together nicely, and at other times pieces seem never to fit; however, when they do fit, the reward is significant.

Nothing in the world can take the place of persistence. Talent will not; nothing is more common than unsuccessful men with talent. Genius will not; heralded genius is almost a proverb. Education will not; the world is full of educated derelicts. Persistence and determination alone are important. Coolidge

12

> *L*eaders are ordinary people
> with extraordinary determination.
>
> ~
>
> *M*en of genius are admired,
> men of wealth are envied, men of power are feared,
> only men of character are trusted.

DEANING

Leo M. Henikoff, MD

$\mathcal{T}$he Wallendas were a family with talents beyond compare. They could walk a tightrope a hundred feet above the ground without fear. Their aerial acrobatics were unparalleled; they could grasp the bar at the only split second when it would be available. When disaster seemed immanent, they could recover their balance and go on as though nothing had happened. We all know that they missed their calling: they should have been medical school deans.

One of their other talents is that when they were in the air, they always knew where they were. Such presence of mind has not always characterized medical deaning or, on occasion, piloting airplanes.

THE FAR SIDE by Gary Larson

"Say . . . what's a mountain goat doing way up here in a cloud bank?"

THE FAR SIDE ©1983 FARWORKS, INC. Used by permission of UNIVERSAL PRESS SYNDICATE.

LEADERSHIP

The single characteristic of deans that is perhaps most important to success is leadership ability. This characteristic supersedes knowledge of finance, management structures, etc. Such knowledge can be learned or bought, but the characteristic of leadership is the critical factor for success. But can leadership be dissected further?

Successful deans must be seen and looked up to as leaders of the faculty. At the same time, they must be seen by presidents of universities as the university official in charge of a large enterprise that must be directed and managed in accordance with the strategic plan of the university. Often the university's goals and objectives differ to a significant degree from those of individual departments within the medical school, and here is the situation in which deans find the tightrope strung 100 feet above the ground.

TRUST

Successful deans must have the trust of the faculty members and of the president. Maintaining that trust in the presence of conflicting goals is the required leadership skill. Loss of trust on either side can mean the demise of the dean. In light of such a conflicting situation and the need for trust, it becomes apparent that the single most important quality of leadership is basic and direct honesty. With the faculty and the university administration so intensely vested in the management of the deanship, any dishonesty will be discovered without question, and trust will be lost. Assuming that the dean would not be dean if the faculty did not believe that a trusting relationship could exist, then the success of the deanship boils down to the dean's relationship with the university president. If that relationship does not work, it is just a matter of time until the deanship is ended or the university enters into a protracted war with its medical school, which creates a destructive rather than a constructive deanship and helps no one.

POWER

The job of dean is inherently a tough one and requires a sense of balance that is demanded nowhere else in the college of medicine. Occasionally the position is doomed from the start because of the university president's position regarding the medical school. For some presidents, the medical school is a crown jewel and a star to be raised. For others, it is an 800-pound gorilla that must be held in check.

Deans are usually seen as powerful people in the university setting, but what really is the source of their power? There is a spectrum of power that goes from political power on one end to earned power on the other, with all shades of gray in between. Because the dean controls a vast array of resources, these resources can be leveraged for political power, much as happens in government. A deanship conducted in this manner invariably runs into difficulty when the available resources for distribution do not meet the needs of the dean for trades in the other direction. In addition, such a deanship falls short in the area of trust (as does the government).

On the other hand, a deanship based on earned power is a deanship that is backed by the trust of the faculty with confidence that the dean's leadership will make the medical school and the individual faculty members more successful. Such power builds upon itself with each success and does not crumble easily.

DEANS AS VIEWED BY OTHERS

Interestingly, deans seem to be viewed differently by students, faculty members, and the public in different parts of the country. Having been a dean for two years in Chicago, I learned quickly that I did not understand the aura of deanship that existed in the East. In my first week as dean at Temple University, I overhead a medical student making an appointment with my secretary to see me at 4:00. When the student came into my office wearing a suit and tie, I was astonished, because I had previously never seen a medical student in a suit and tie. I asked him very innocently where he was going. When he responded, "to see you," I realized that I had made a rather large mistake!

On the other hand, in the East, deans, although revered, were believed by the very nature of their position to be inept at clinical medicine. In Chicago I had been a very active pediatric cardiologist with a particular love for the catheterization laboratory. It was assumed when I arrived at Temple that my absurd request to have such privileges would lead to recurrent and immediate patient deaths in the cardiac catheterization laboratory and must be avoided at all costs! I didn't understand why it took so long for me to obtain privileges!

However, when the deans of the other colleges of Temple University welcomed me to the fold in an impressive ceremony somewhat akin to crossing the equator for the first time at sea, I understood. The following is a direct quote from the diploma that I received at that ceremony:

"Know all men by these predicaments that Leo M. Henikoff has been admitted to the Council of Deans at Temple University with all the lack of privileges, denial of rights, and burdening of responsibilities expected by every other dean; that he shall henceforth have his scholarship scorned by the faculty and his reputation derided by the students, who shall consider him a person of great rank and low esteem; moreover, he shall patiently suffer the violent demands and mournful entreaties of his department chairmen for more staff, larger programs, and greater expenses while gently turning his cheek to an administration that threatens fewer staff, smaller programs, and no expenses, to this end he must cheerfully endorse rapid promotions for the pearls of this faculty, recommending their frequent leave from the campus with ample funds for contemplative study, yet himself persevering throughout the year on the psychic income of joyful student counseling, stimulating faculty conferences, and the never-ending excitement of the administration's agenda; although his faculty may consider him an academic renegade and an intellectual eunuch, to the public he shall appear as a benevolent sage and to the administration as an educational philosopher, capable of Socratic speech whether dealing with an incomprehensible curriculum, budgetary deficits, student turmoil, or ruptured air-conditioning; may his health be perfect and his family forgiving as he enters this condemned circle!"

Never speak ill of yourself, others will always say enough on that subject.

I understand that we are now using lawyers for research instead of rats. Lawyers are more plentiful, technicians don't get attached to lawyers and there are some things that rats just won't do.

13

*T*he first law of political leadership,
find out where the people want to go
then hustle yourself around in front of them.

ROLE OF THE DEAN
AND FACULTY
IN GOVERNANCE
OF THE MEDICAL SCHOOL*

John R. Hogness, MD

* Excerpts from JAMA May 27, 1968

$\mathcal{W}$e need only look at the turnover rate of deans of medical schools to realize that something is amiss. The average dean is not totally happy in his job. This unhappiness arises in part because of the pressures put on him from many sources, but it also arises because he is usually untrained for the role he must play. Further, as soon as he leaves the fold of the faculty and assumes the mantle of dean, he is invested in the eyes of the faculty with a strange and wonderful aura. Edward Rosenheim, Jr., professor of English at the University of Chicago, has written a classic "Letter to a New Dean."[1] Addressing his friend Fats, the new Dean of Floodwater State University, Rosenheim comments:

> You are, of course, an amiable and humble man; beware, however, the illusion that the deanship involves a subtle, special expertise, the mastery of a craft whose dark secrets are unknown to your faculty colleagues, a solitary struggle with esoteric problems we cannot understand. This view of the deanship is poppycock. One becomes an academic administrator because, in the Country of the Blind, the one-eyed man is king. A qualified academic administrator is only a professor who answers his mail.

Pressures and the lack of administrative preparation are only part of the problem. The medical school dean also faces problems common to many aspects of our society, problems well expressed by two distinguished men, educator John Gardner[2] and journalist James Reston. In "The Antileadership Vaccine," Gardner writes:

> The confidence required of leaders poses a delicate problem for a free society. We don't want to be led by Men of Destiny who think they know all of the answers. Neither do we wish to be led by Nervous Nellies. It is a matter of balance. We are no longer in much danger, in this society, from Men of Destiny. But we are in danger of falling under the leadership of men who lack the confidence to lead.

In one of his newspaper columns (*Seattle Post-Intelligencer,* May 4, 1966), Reston points out,

> "There is a problem here…it is not merely a problem of what to do but deciding how to decide what to do."

These points seem to me central, and bearing them in mind, I believe that we should look at the present organization of the academic medical center. What is its relationship to the rest of the university? What is the role of the dean? What is the dean's relationship to the vice president, when there is one? What is the role of the chairs and of the faculty members in the administration of the center?

THE ACADEMIC MEDICAL CENTER

Over the course of the last twenty or thirty years, and particularly in the last ten years, medical schools have been converted to academic medical centers. Before World War II, the main function of medical schools was to train medical students. In some instances, but by no means all, a modest amount of research was conducted, usually by a small full-time faculty nucleus in the basic science departments. Sources of revenue were relatively straightforward, and a single mission was easily defined.

There has been a dramatic change in the scope of activity of the medical school, both academic and nonacademic, so that it has now become a complex center with a budget many times larger than that of its predecessor, the medical school. New teaching programs, graduate education, postdoctoral education, house-staff training, vast research programs, education for the ever-increasing allied health professions, and continuing education programs have been added. There are new responsibilities for the administration of hospitals, of institutes and centers, and of interdepartmental training programs.

The social changes that affect the medical center are emerging so rapidly that the programs they create are often handled in a haphazard, uncoordinated fashion. Such a disjointed approach to the management of the varied external and internal programs of the center can no longer be tolerated. And yet it is the very attempt to coordinate, to regulate, and to shift priorities that is producing significant stress within our institutions.

RELATIONSHIP OF THE
MEDICAL SCHOOL TO THE UNIVERSITY

By and large, the medical school of the past was marked by its separateness from its parent university. This circumstance came about because of the uniqueness and now the increasing complexity of the activities within the medical center, and because of the size of its budget as compared with other schools and colleges of the university. Also, it must be admitted that it has come about because deans and medical school faculties preferred it that way, and because many university administrators and nonmedical faculty members were more comfortable that way. I believe that the continued separation of medical centers from their parent universities is deleterious to the programs and activities of both. The medical center must become an integral part of the university, a university which itself is changing dramatically in scope, concept, and mission. New interdisciplinary programs such as bioengineering, research in systems of health care, community medicine, biomedical history, biomathematics, and behavioral sciences depend upon cooperation between faculties of various parts of the university. These programs cannot be developed successfully unless faculties from different university disciplines can work together conveniently. The umbrella of the university is important if the medical center is to maintain academic standards, resist outside pressures, and help the leadership of the medical center identify pertinent social and educational problems. The university can and should be the cohesive force that helps in the establishment and maintenance of patterns of administration within the center. The forceful backing of a strong, informed president and central administration is basic to the readjustments that the modern academic medical center is experiencing.

In more than half of the existing medical centers in the United States, a relatively new administrative officer has been added to the hierarchy, somewhere between the president and the deans of the health-related schools. Most often this person is designated a vice president, although a number of other titles are used. This new office has been created because of the increasing complexity of the academic medical center and the resultant need to coordinate the academic programs in the increasing number of health professions and their respective schools and colleges. Sometimes this position has been created to relieve the enormous burden that is borne by the dean of the school of medicine. There can be no question that the trend today is to create more of these offices in modern universities. This new administrative pattern has worked well in some instances and less well in others, depending upon personalities and whether the respective roles of the vice president and the dean are clearly defined in advance of appointment and whether, once defined, the division of responsibility is respected by the two parties as well as by the president of the university and the faculty members. In all instances in which a vice president and a dean of a medical school are present in the same organization, it must be clear that the vice president acts for the president in the administration of the university and is not responsible for the day-to-day or year-to-year operation of the medical school. The dean, on the other hand, is responsible to the vice-president in the same fashion as he was formerly responsible to the president.

Further, it must be recognized that the creation of the office of vice president, or its equivalent, may well relieve the president of some burdens, but, by and in itself, it does not contribute much to the relief of the administrative burden experienced by the dean of the school of medicine. A solution for the latter problem must be found in more effective organization within the dean's office and the departmental structure of the medical school, permitting better long-range planning and more delegation of responsibility down the administrative ladder.

ROLE OF THE DEAN

The modern academic medical center, like its parent university, is not a democracy. It is rather a responsible oligarchy, with the administration subject to certain checks and balances in the area of academic programs and responsible for its actions to a higher university authority and, to a degree, to society. The dean is called upon, from time to time, to be a mediator and a diplomat, but, again quoting from Edward Rosenheim,[1] "Far more frequently the dean is called upon to be an advocate, a defender, a spokesman, an enforcer, an innovator-in short a leader." To paraphrase Rosenheim, deans have an obligation to lead. In so doing they also have an obligation to make known to their faculty members their long-range goals and to pursue them openly. When deans must be politicians, as often they must and should, their political activities should be open and the convictions on which these activities are based should be plainly understood. Deans must ride herd and nag; they should teach and ask questions. They must stir up within the faculty a state of doubt that leads to inquiry, and make clear that doubt and inquiry are the proper conditions of the intellectual. Deans are responsible for maintaining balance and strength within the institution. They must assure that opposing views are compromised or at least modified, and that one powerful influence within the school does not overwhelm another less aggressive but equally important one.

In addition to the power of their own personalities, deans have at their disposal three primary areas of authority that permit them to exert influence on the policy and programs of the institution and to direct it in the path they believe to be right. They have the responsibility for the assignment of space within the institution, control over school-wide committee appointments (an important means of influencing policy and program), and authority to appoint and discharge department chairmen. Deans usually seek the advice of the faculty members, often obtained through department chairs, before wielding their authority. But the final responsibility and authority, within the confines of the school, rest with the dean.

DECISION-MAKING AND DELEGATION OF AUTHORITY

Leadership requires decision making. In a large institution, proper implementation of decisions requires delegation of authority. The decision-making process in many academic medical centers is poorly defined and poorly understood. All too often, decisions are made on an ad hoc basis without reference to a long-range plan. In these increasingly complex yet in some ways increasingly predictable times, a workable mechanism for long-range planning is essential. Unfortunately, although there are signs of change, few if any academic medical centers now have such a mechanism. All too often, long-range concepts, if there are any, are carried in the dean's head. With the fields of biology and medicine changing rapidly, and with the crescendo of public concern about medical care, a planning and evaluation office within the medical center is a must.

Despite advice that dates back at least to the time of Moses, many of us find it difficult to delegate authority.

Deans should appoint an appropriate and adequate number of assistant and associate deans, business officers, and senior nonacademic staff members. Deans must clearly define the areas of responsibility of these appointees and should delegate appropriate decision-making powers to them and to department chairs. This delegation is often difficult. Everybody wants to talk to the dean. Furthermore, the dean is often overly sensitive to snide comments about "burgeoning administrative bureaucracy." The fact remains, however, that a large administrative structure is necessary to run a large enterprise. Without adequate administrative personnel, the entire institution suffers, and the dean's life becomes intolerable.

The job of a dean is a lonely one. Rosenheim[1] writes, "I suspect a great dean is rarely a popular and comfortable one." Those who survive are those who are able to accept this fact with reasonable equanimity. The job requires more than an average degree of self assurance, even egocentricity, but it is always challenging, usually exciting, often rewarding, and never dull.

The modern academic medical center is an enormous, rapidly changing, unwieldy, vibrant and active, often aggressive, sometimes insecure collection of individual entrepreneurs, theoretically held together and sometimes led by an entrepreneur-coordinator, usually referred to politely as a dean. The fundamental problem confronting those of us concerned with the administration of this center is to establish a decision-making process that allows a response to new and anticipated programs and will at the same time mesh with the university tradition of academic independence and academic excellence - excellent students, excellent curricula, excellent facilities, and, above all, an excellent faculty.

References:

1. Rosenheim, E., Jr.: "Letter to a New Dean," *Amer Assoc Univ Prof Bull*, autumn 1963, pp 226-231,
2. Gardner, J.W.: "The Antileadership Vaccine," in *Annual Report Carnegie Corporation of New York*, 1963, pp 3-12,

Jones' Laws:

The person who can smile when things go wrong has thought of someone to blame it on.

It does no good to leave a live dragon out of your calculations if you live near him.

When you are in trouble try to keep your chin up and your mouth shut.

Snap judgments tend to have a talent for coming unfastened at the worst possible moment.

People are given a mouth that closes and ears that don't, which should tell us something.

14

> "*No* one would remember the good samaritan if he'd only had good intentions; he had money too."
>
> Margaret Thatcher

SUCCESS AND LONGEVITY IN THE DEANSHIP

Richard Janeway, MD

$\mathcal{M}$uch of this article will sound as if it was pirated from Robert Fulghum - "Everything I needed to know to be a dean, I learned in kindergarten!" Some of the elements that enable successful longevity in the Deanship are structurally based in the institution, and others are quirks of circumstance, either controllable or uncontrollable. Some elements are rooted in personality characteristics and personal qualifications, two very different but closely related attributes. Many other elements are basic principles of management and leadership.

STRUCTURAL REQUIREMENTS

To speak first of structural elements, there are certain basic authorities:
- controlling the budget, including unrestricted funds, and oversight of the medical service plan;
- appointing chairs and committees;
- allocating space;
- influencing directly the rubric of education; and
- structuring your administration as you see fit.

These are the tools needed to do the two most important things a dean must do: refine the institutional culture, and set the tone for institutional betterment.

QUIRKS OF CIRCUMSTANCE

Controllable quirks, like politics, are local. There are, however, quirks of circumstance that are uncontrollable. I shall mention only one:

If there has been a string of short-term Deans before you, don't expect to last long. There are no prophets out there predicting that you are the Messiah.

$\mathcal{S}$ome folks say the squeaking wheel gets the grease but others point out that it is the first one to be replaced.

PERSONAL CHARACTERISTICS AND CAPABILITIES

I believe that certain personal characteristics and capabilities are found in most successful deans. Personal characteristics include the following:
- a high tolerance for ambiguity;
- a sense of humor, particularly about one's own foibles;
- a minimal need for short-term reward;
- broad shoulders without chips;
- a strong sense of self-worth, which means that one must have ego strength without ego; and
- the ability to listen.

Basic capabilities include the following:
- the ability to articulate a vision in a convincing and consistent fashion;
- a superior capacity to select personnel;
- skills in problem identification and conflict resolution;
- a conceptual understanding of space and money;
- the ability to create the readiness to change;
- the courage to make unpopular decisions; and
- an IQ greater than 100.

SELECTION OF CHAIRS

One of the first realities you have to face is that chairs don't want to manage, but they don't want to be managed. Management skill is not a paramount consideration for search committees.

Chairs must have many of the personal characteristics and capabilities that I identified as important for deans. When looking for a chair, I try to follow one rule, having adopted it from a guy named Peterson who ran AVIS: "If you are more than 50% sure that an internal candidate can do the job, you had better pick that person. If you are right more than 50% of the time on outside candidates, you are just plain lucky."

Let's start with what I won't tolerate in a chair: a department chair who solves departmental problems by sending them to the dean's office. Chairs have every right to expect that I will do my best to manage institutional change while maintaining institutional stability. I have every right to expect chairs to solve their own problems. The president expects me to solve medical school problems.

In appropriate forums, I expect chairs to negotiate, and sometimes purely to bargain, in the perceived self-interest of a department constituency. When institutional interests are involved, however, I expect chairs to participate as problem solvers who can see beyond the narrow confines of a department or specialty to achieve a broader, and, yes, a more important goal.

I convey to chairs that they are expected to balance their personal and departmental orientations between a cosmopolitan extramural presence reflecting specialty loyalty and excellence and the more parochial role reflecting a high level of institutional participation. In other words, a chair must understand that the endowed chair is at home and not on United Airlines.

I want a chair who understands the concept that "We are in this together." Show me a dean who thinks of "my" chairs, or a chair who thinks in terms of "my" faculty, and I will show you a person who will enjoy only a limited tenure of administrative service. It is "our school," not theirs, not mine. Recruit the best people you can, agree upon a plan, and then get out of the way. Miracles are more likely to occur if they are preceded by planning and preparation.

> *As dean, there are times when you feel like you are wrestling a bear, but you cannot get tired. You have to wait until the bear gets tired.*

MAXIMS

I have tried to live by certain maxims. I recognize that these guideposts are replete with contradiction, but in my opinion, contradiction is descriptive of the dean's job. That is why you must have a high tolerance for ambiguity.

Here are five maxims that speak to the centrality of education:
• The only unique thing about medical schools is that we educate medical students. Medical students are the only people in the institution who are paying for the privilege of being there. If students didn't show up every year, we'd be out of a job and have to go to work. Remind faculty members of this fact with metronomic regularity.
• See a student anytime and a member of the faculty if at all possible; require chairs to make an appointment.
• Students under pressure are not the world's most objective critics. Students think they are always under pressure. Treat them like colleagues so that they learn what real pressure is.
• Instill an institutional reverence for scholarship, whether it be related to research, teaching, or clinical care: show your reverence by the way you allocate money as well as by the way you allocate your mouth. Research funded by institutional dollars gets no stars in heaven: remind the faculty members of their reciprocal responsibility to the institution.
• Regardless of *U.S. News and World Report,* the long-term performance of your graduates will be the ultimate determinant of your school's reputation.

At the personal level, I have tried to live by another set of maxims:
• The job of the dean is to help other people's dreams come true.
• Make sure you have an office with a side door. You have to spend a lot of time swimming with sharks, and if you get bitten don't bleed. Go to the "other guy's" office for meetings. This puts you in charge of your own time expenditure.
• Get a private toilet: it will save you an hour a day. If you have your own private toilet, you won't be in the hallway when you don't want to be. Make no hallway promises.
• Wear your identification tag. If you don't, nobody else will.

• Make as many of your own phone calls as you can. Don't get upset when the secretary to the chair of surgery asks you to spell your name and wants you to identify your institutional affiliation. Don't get upset when the hospital director is "in an all-day meeting." That's what hospital directors do.

• Make sure your best friends are outside the medical center. Prepare your spouse not to get upset when she is shunned by the spouse of a faculty member you have censured, or even mildly criticized. Your outside friends won't shun you. Nobody in the outside world has tenure, and they are used to constructive criticism.

• Pick a non-medical mentor who knows how to manage. Success breeds success, and your mentor probably accepted some constructive criticism along the way.

• Remember that praise, should you get any, is like after-shave lotion: it makes you tingle and feel good all over, but if you swallow it, it will kill you. You won't get much praise; faculty members definitely are not praise-givers the way patients are. In their own opinion, faculty members are not the least bit like patients: don't let them in on your secret knowledge of their human failings.

• If you begin to trip over your shoelaces, consider retirement: lawyers wear tasseled loafers and, hence, trip less often.

• Remind yourself occasionally that whoever "they" are, "they" didn't force the job on you. Find out who "they," that is, the Search Committee, were. Ignore them: they have a vested interest in your success.

• You have to believe in what you do to convince others to invest in your school. If you don't believe, nobody else will. When you are out raising money for the school, do it forcefully: you are not raising money for yourself. Don't play "poor us": people want to invest in winners.

Certain management principles are also important:

• Always try to do what is right: it will gratify some of the faculty and astonish the rest. In other words, never give up the moral high ground. If you lie down with dogs, you will get up with fleas. Remember the plague.

• Never rise up more snakes than you can conveniently kill at one time. Rome wasn't built in a day, but it sure as hell burned in one. Also remember that, regardless of mythology, there have never been any snakes in Ireland. In most circumstances, fact will triumph over fiction.

• Always tell the faculty what you are going to do and why you are going to do it. Then do it! Be prepared to explain what you have done and why you did it. Don't be defensive. You shouldn't be offensive too often, but occasionally it really helps, especially if you do it on a topic when there is no other real choice, like a federal law. I call this "invoking the Martians." If this fails, hire a Martian, an alien most people call a "consultant."

• Remember that being dean is like being executive director of a cemetery: you have thousands of people under you, but nobody listens to you.

• Before you take a "no back down" stand on an issue, make sure you are prepared for it to be your last stand. You can compromise without being compromised. However, most of the time you should decide quickly: 85% of the time, you will have a "gut" feeling of what is right. Decide immediately. Just don't fall in love with your decision. Second thoughts come mostly when it is too late to use them. If experience proves you are wrong, admit it, and change course. You might even have to hire a Martian.

• Never accept a petition. Never try to teach a pig to sing. It's a waste of time - and it will annoy the pig.

• Never confuse power and authority. Power is an imputed phenomenon. Power is gained by not using it. Power is not like sex: if you use power too often, you lose it. Sex has a lot more to recommend it than does power.

• Never gripe down. Don't kick your dog, either: he has sharper teeth than you do.

• Stay "home" as much as you can. The faculty members, even the chairs, want you to make the hard decisions. They will blame you anyway whether you decide or not.

• Don't be worried about not making enough decisions. An important dimension of leadership is not necessarily how many decisions you make, but the extent to which your ideas get incorporated into the decisions of others.

• Create "disciples in residence." Good things happen most often when someone else has an idea that he thinks is his. Never let on that it was your idea in the first place. You can accomplish anything if you don't care who gets the credit.

• Immediately fire any chair who writes a contentious memo to you and sends a blind copy to the president of the university (or to anyone else, for that matter). He who hesitates with the scalpel leaves ugly-looking scars.

• Encourage the faculty to do what they are capable of doing. If you expect excellence out of people and convey that message to them, they will do what they are capable of doing. If you do not, they will remain as they are: inertia rules.

• A faculty member is aptly described as "someone who thinks otherwise." Don't ever forget that you used to be a faculty member. You think you still are, but "they" don't. Even paranoids can have real enemies. Console yourself with the realization that it is more important that the dean be trusted than liked.

• Don't ever specialize in anything. Surround yourself with people who do. They will continue to teach you. God willing, you will continue to learn from them.

• Move your best people around and test their capabilities to become successor management. If we did a better job of this, there would be less turnover in the dean's office. On the other hand, more people will want your job, and the turnover that occurs will at least have a more rational basis. It might even improve the organization.

• Recruit faculty members who are brighter than their predecessors. This should get more difficult as time goes on. Recruit people to management who are brighter than you are: this should be easy. It will be if you reward their excellence, and get the hell out of their way.

• Never equivocate with a surgeon. Any first-class surgeon will pay you for the privilege of operating. Our surgeons do it every day, and they only gripe down. At the same time, I warn you not to get surgically sick until after you have retired and become the "beloved old dean."

• If you don't already understand money, take a course: take a lot of courses if you have graduated from medical school. I would hope that you know that decision-making is easier if you are independently wealthy.

• Memorize the faculty handbook and then burn all copies. Best of all, write the handbook yourself and make no copies. I wrote ours. I didn't burn the copies, but as far as I know, I am the only person who has read the whole thing, my assistant excepted.

• Never depend on a majority vote on important issues: horizontal organizations don't work that way. Better yet, don't vote on anything.

• The dean who will deceive his faculty in public will eventually deceive himself in private.

• Do LCME accreditation site visits and get active in the AAMC. Both of these efforts will make you happy that you are where you are. At the same time, informed people who get recruited away from your school to "better" positions have created the "second-best" outcome. They have reaffirmed your judgment of their value.

• Competition in industry is dog-eat-dog. Remember that in academic medicine it is just the opposite.

• Manage by walking around. You can't identify an inactive lab while sitting in your office. Get to know everybody on the custodial staff by name: they will tell you what's going on. Don't rat on them or they will unionize, and you will have no source of absolute truth.

• Active participation in the university senate is inversely correlated with academic productivity.

• The worst time to disagree with your boss is when you are in the right.

• A dean has to be like a tea bag: you produce stronger tea when you are put in hot water.

• While you are killing alligators, try to remember that presumably you were elected to drain the swamp. Don't remind the alligators you are killing of the reasons therefore: just make sure they are dead. A word of caution: I have learned that with most alligators, reincarnation may be inevitable. Before you kill an alligator, check first to see that you are covered by the university's director and officer liability policy. If not, move to the Grand Caymans.

• Don't accept a low salary out of institutional loyalty or a sense of personal guilt. You were not elected to be a martyr, and everyone knows you are not a saint. At the same time, don't be jealous of the incomes of clinical faculty. No matter what your income, be at your happiest when an assistant professor of molecular genetics shows up in a chauffeured Rolls- Royce: the institution just got rich, too.

• Never promise more than you can deliver. Never reduce a promise to a spreadsheet.

• Never say never. Even if your will expresses an absolute aversion to cremation, you won't be there to cast the deciding vote.

And finally, there are 10 simple truths, most of which, in contrast to the Ten Commandments, are positives:

1. Don't commit your calendar without first asking your administrative assistant if it's okay. Good administrative assistants are hard to find. I know one who survived the tenure of six deans.

2. Always make friends with the facts. You can't create an infinite supply of needles by creating an infinite number of haystacks.

3. Always praise in public and criticize only in private.

4. If you and the hospital director agree on everything, there is a high probability that you are both wrong.

5. Relish the inadequacy of facilities: if you don't have a space problem, you are dead in the water.

6. Orthopedic surgeons are made of bone from the big toe to the sagittal suture. Your future is not destined by the fact that they are strong as an ox and half as smart.

7. Never appoint a committee to recommend allocation of the space.

8. Handle with good humor the fact that no good deed shall go unpunished. If you get stuck, don't squeal. Scars have the curious capacity to remind us that our past is real.

9. Make time for your family. That's where you live.

10. Try to solve problems that have solutions: have all parking decisions made by the president of the university.

In the final analysis, personal attitudes and behaviors determine success or failure. You must place your happiness in life beyond your institutional life. In short, if you "need" your job, or if it isn't fun, get out of it.

I have undoubtedly left out some of the really important things that ought to be on this list, probably because I have been doing this job for so long that I have forgotten the most important things. Keep one watchword: espouse the attitude expressed by Stark Draper of the instrumentation labs at MIT: if you really want to lead, don't ask the faculty members to give the school all the years of their lives - just the best ones.

*T*he negotiation process is a compromising process. As Moses said descending the mountain, "Well, I got him down to ten, but he wants to keep the one on adultery in there."

15

> *I*gnorance can get you into trouble;
> arrogance keeps you there.

DEANING AND ACADEMIC ADMINISTRATION

Michael M.E. Johns, MD

It is tempting to start this essay with some sort of amusing anecdote or analogy, because much that occurs within the province of a medical school deanship is humorous - especially in hindsight! However, I think I should start from the beginning; and from beginning to end what animated and suffused all of my experience as a medical school dean was the sense of awe and responsibility that assuming this position represented.

Having and sustaining such a sense is the first prerequisite for success in the position of dean. The day that you wake up and think to yourself, "Boy, this job is for the birds!" is the day that you should initiate the search for your successor. It turns out that this day has dawned earlier and earlier for deans across the country. When I attended an AAMC Council of Deans meeting during the third year of my deanship, the subject was the short average tenure of medical school deans - at that point, about 3.6 years. The discussion centered on all of the things that put a dean at risk:

- being too aggressive in attempting reforms,
- being too shy in attempting reforms,
- involving the faculty too closely in a variety of administrative affairs,
- not involving the faculty enough in administrative affairs, and
- university administrations from their medical schools not pushing hard enough to bridge such chasms.

At that moment the difficulty of succeeding as a dean became crystal clear to me. Especially in times of change and uncertainty, it is very hard to find reliable rules or guidelines for leadership. When change is happening, the leadership required will vary to a great extent depending upon the particular circumstances at each institution. Having said that, I have found in my experience that certain qualities are particularly helpful to leaders in a changing environment.

AWE AND RESPONSIBILITY

The first quality is the one I began with: a true sense of awe and responsibility. The awe relates to being asked to provide leadership for people - your faculty members - who are among the brightest and most dedicated in the world. If you don't feel and believe that sense of awe going in, then you are at risk of being undermined by arrogance: either your own or that of your faculty. The sense of responsibility too must be there: the sense that leadership is now your job. This sense of responsibility means meeting and exceeding not only your own expectations but also those of the faculty. In a time of change, conducting yourself simply as a caretaker or an executor, simply following a given set of rules or customs - or acting as a lone ranger or rescuer, determined to completely revolutionize the existing order - will ensure that your tenure falls well below the median. Leadership in an era of change requires, first of all, humility and openness to a great deal of input.

VISION: SEEING THE WHOLE PLAYING FILED

The second quality required, regardless of the particulars of the situation, is vision. What I mean is vision with a small "v" much more than with the big "V." Vision in this sense refers to the capacity and the drive to see the whole playing field, to be the person primarily responsible for continuously taking in the whole of the changing landscape and the changing players within and around it. If your vision is too narrowly focused on one aspect or pet project, or if your vision is so grandiose that you lose sight of the individual players and their needs, your institution will lose its capacity to plan well for the future. Lacking vision is another characteristic that will ensure that your tenure is below the median.

PROBLEMS AND SOLUTIONS

A third quality that also appears to be essential in a changing environment is a passion for taking on problems and finding solutions. I have been introduced to others on more than one occasion as someone who "has never seen a problem he didn't like." I would ascribe this characteristic to all of the successful medical school and other leaders I have known. If you don't get up in the morning excited about the issues and challenges you face, but instead feel overwhelmed by them, you will not do well. It is time to step aside.

NO SURPRISES

One must be committed to expanding the number of chairs at the planning and decision-making table. In a time of significant challenges, the last thing a faculty needs or wants is surprises from its leadership. The process of creating and ensuring buy-in must be of the highest priority. This means bringing an ever-expanding number of key faculty members into the entire spectrum of issues and decisions facing the institution - and from the earliest possible moment.

IDENTIFY THE BEST AND BRIGHTEST

Fifth, but by no means least in order of importance, a good leader must be willing and able to bring to the leadership team the best and brightest. This means having the confidence to seek out and work with people who know more than you do, who may be smarter than you are and who may have very different perspectives than you do. It is impossible to steer and sail such a large and complex vessel as a medical school all by yourself. You need a top-quality team to handle something so vast and unwieldy. Failure to recruit such a team will land you on the rocks sooner rather than later.

IT IS NOT WHAT ONE UNDERTAKES BUT HOW ONE UNDERTAKES IT

During the Council of Deans meeting I described earlier, more than one colleague insisted that the surest road to a short and unsuccessful tenure as dean was to attempt to revise the medical school curriculum. I suppose it's a good thing I hadn't heard that a couple of years earlier, because that was exactly the first thing I undertook. Over a period of four years, our curriculum was very successfully and very substantially revised. The success of this undertaking can be attributed 95% to the buy-in and subsequent leadership of key faculty members, both clinical and basic science faculty members, that we achieved from the beginning. The buy-in came not simply in the formulation of a new curriculum, but before that, in the evaluation of the existing curriculum.

Financial issues are another well-known cause of deanship mortality, especially when the issues are where and how much to cut spending. My approach was to put the administrative team to work to solicit and find the best fifteen proposals to achieve the correct budget. Long sessions were devoted to working with faculty leadership so that they would understand the finances of the school of medicine. Then we met with all of the faculty leaders and asked them to choose what they thought were the best options or to propose others that we might not have seen. We were able to attain agreement and buy-in on a plan and a process by which to achieve our goals.

From these experiences, I believe the lesson is that it's not what one undertakes as a leader, so much as how one undertakes it, that determines one's chances of success in leading such vital and complex organizations.

DIFFICULTIES AND FAILURES

All of this is not to suggest that my tenure as dean was without its difficulties and failures. Particularly difficult was managing the relationship with our affiliated hospital, where differences in priorities, culture, and management style existed. The relationship was such that it often felt to me as if we were like two very large vessels tied together on leads that gave each only minimal room for maneuver, all in the midst of a very large and unabating gale-force storm. Even though we were sailing in the same direction, the facts of our separate relationship with two "captains" accountable to two different boards meant we were often in danger of colliding, as one and then the other of us attempted to make course corrections according to our perceived and anticipated circumstances and needs.

From my perspective now as the leader of an integrated academic health system, I would say that it is far better to have a single organization with all the components under one leader and one leadership organization. The leadership team needs to be larger, and many issues still are difficult to resolve, but under one skipper there is a better opportunity for timely and clear resolution.

The last decade has been an especially challenging time for leadership of medical schools and academic health centers. It is very difficult to reconcile the forces unleashed by the advent of managed care, an economic climate that requires a pulling-in of spending, and an environment in medicine and health care that is straining to push out new priorities and develop new capabilities.

LEADERSHIP WITH A SENSE OF HONOR

More than ever before, we need leadership with the qualities necessary to manage large and complex enterprises - extraordinary institutions dedicated to teaching, scholarship, and research, and to protecting and advancing the health of individuals and populations; institutions with diverse constituencies, multiple needs, and great aspirations. The qualities outlined are those most necessary for success in these stormy seas, although there is one other: a sense of humor. Though somewhat reluctant to begin this essay with humor, I will end with it.

For a dean, it is often the medical students who are the greatest source of humor and perspective, which is one reason why it is important to stay close to the students. One day I awoke early on a Friday morning to find my kitchen full of medical students, my son among them, preparing to go off on a long skiing weekend. A bit surprised by the nonchalance of these students in preparing to cut classes in full view of their dean, I made a not-too-subtle inquiry concerning their plans. As they explained their itinerary, I interjected a query to the effect of, "Aren't you at all concerned that you are setting off on this adventure - and skipping classes - in full view of me?" They all glanced at one another and then one of them replied, "Nah. We wouldn't do this in front of a professor, but you're only the dean."

I could only smile and laugh, grateful for the youthful candor and perspective. As goes your sense of humor, so goes your tenure in leadership of academic medicine.

The fellow who says he will meet you half-way usually thinks he is standing on the dividing line.

~

"Diplomacy is the art of allowing someone else to have your own way." Daniele Vare

~

When arguing with a stupid person be sure that he/she isn't doing the same.

~

Beware of half truths; you may have gotten hold of the wrong half.

16

> *D*on't ever slam a door, you may want to go back in.
>
> ~
>
> *The* *Deans'* *L*ament
>
> *The world is divided between*
> *victims and predators*
> *and you have to defend yourself against both.*

REFLECTIONS

Richard H. Moy, MD

*H*aving been a dean for more than 23 years, I have accumulated a few insights from my own experience and from watching my fellow deans. No one goes to medical school to be a dean; thus, we track into that calling for a variety of reasons. In my case it started when I was chief resident in medicine at the University of Chicago. To my surprise, I found that I enjoyed administration and particularly the ability to make small reforms in the educational experiences of medical students and residents.

As I advanced in the faculty, my interests in educational reform grew, but the ability to make larger changes in an established institution was limited. Thus, to be offered at the age of 38 the opportunity to start a new medical school was irrepressible.

During the first several years, while building up the school, I had to request quite a few new procedures, titles, contracting authority, and various exceptions to the university's usual way of doing business. After a particularly complicated request got through the Board of Trustees, I commented to the academic vice president how much I appreciated the Board's going along with all of my requests. He replied that they had thought about this quite a bit but, realizing that none of them knew about medical schools, they decided to do it my way until I blew it, and then they would fire me.

REFLECTIONS

• A medical school is not just another academic program in the university. It is very different; it is out in the real world of medicine and complicated economics, and it is critical that the president and the trustees understand this.

• The best position is that of a vice president or dean who reports directly to the president. The most fatal position is to have the title of dean, while all the chairmen really report to the vice president for health affairs who was the former dean. This is a kamikaze flight unless you are really what in most schools would be called "an associate dean for academic affairs." Your authority must match your accountability.

• Don't be afraid to fire people. Successful deans are respected and even liked by some, but don't expect to be loved or you will fail. Decisions must be made, and some of them are hard. A medical school is a human enterprise, and some people just don't work out. Once you are convinced of that statement, deal with problems, and don't be surprised when the same person who says in public that you are a mean SOB for what you did tells you in private that you did the right thing. In recognizing my retirement, the chairman of surgery said that one of my strongest attributes was that I made decisions. Rare praise, indeed, from a surgeon to an internist.

• Hire MBA assistants for all departmental chairmen and associate deans. I knew that as a community-based medical school we would be getting into very complicated financial and management relationships. These kind of smarts do not ordinarily come with the MD degree.

• Now that you have everyone's respect (or fear), it's time to lighten up. Keep your sense of humor, and particularly don't take yourself too seriously. For many years as I telephoned people around the school, a secretary would say "May I tell him who's calling?" I would reply, "This is the glorious leader." The usual response was a chuckle followed by, "Yes, Dr. Moy, I'll tell him you're on the line." One day, when calling one of our professors, I gave this line to a new secretary. After a long pause, she said, "Yes, Mr. Leader, I'll tell him you're on the line." After a short time the professor came on the line laughing and said, "Dick, you'll have to be careful using that line when you call the department of psychiatry."

MOY'S LAWS

We were quite successful in recruiting from business and state government people with the required credentials, but it became quickly obvious that virtually none of them had any experience working around MDs or researchers. Thus, after several years I came up with Moy's Laws for the introduction of business people to a medical school.

• IF THERE IS A POSSIBLE SOURCE
OF CONFUSION, IT WILL BE FOUND.

Professional managers in medical schools should be very cautious about making assumptions about how much the faculty members and chairs understand about management and administrative procedures.

• FOR PROFESSIONAL MANAGERS
IN MEDICAL SCHOOLS,
THEIR HIGHEST COMPLIMENT
IS TO BE TAKEN FOR GRANTED.

Management services is something like dormitory food. If nobody is complaining, you are a spectacular success.

• IN ACADEMIC MEDICINE,
IF YOUR BASTARDS ARE GOOD ENOUGH,
YOU CALL THEM ECCENTRIC.

There are some faculty members who are so brilliant or productive that you simply have to put up with their irritating behavior and make the system work for them in spite of your homicidal impulses. If you like golden eggs, do not develop a taste for goose.

• MEDICAL SCHOOLS DO NOT EXIST
FOR THE PURPOSE OF HOLDING
MANAGEMENT SERVICES.

Medical schools are primarily educational institutions that must be supported by management services. Employees, particularly those from a business background with profit incentives, sometimes cannot appreciate this.

• MATURE BEHAVIOR IS DIRECTLY
PROPORTIONAL TO GRUBBINESS OF HANDS.

All doctors wash their hands, and surgeons scrub them. When professional managers are dealing with faculty members, particularly clinical faculty members, it is important to remember that some of their behavioral attributes relate to things that they do at other times when they are not talking to professional managers.

• ALL FUNDING SOURCES
CATEGORICALLY ASSUME
THAT THEY ARE PAYING MORE
THAN THEIR SHARE.

This fact of necessity creates the need for cost accounting, which unfortunately is a source of great irritation to most faculty members.

• A BIRD IN THE HAND
MAY LEAVE DROPPINGS IN YOUR PALM.

It is sometimes best not to fill vacant positions from inside the institution.

• IF YOU GO OUT TO SMITE PHILISTINES
WITH THE JAW BONE OF AN ASS,
BE SURE IT'S NOT YOUR JAW BONE.

Deaning can be very rewarding, but for the most part you have to take the long view. Most important projects take time, so your rewards are more like those of a pediatrician than of a surgeon. However, when the going is slow and it seems that nobody cares, remember Preston's Law (that is, Sergeant Preston of the Yukon and his mighty dog, King): "THE LEAD DOG DOES MOST OF THE WORK, BUT THEN HE'S THE ONLY ONE WITH THE VIEW."

"You can fool some of the people all of the time and all of the people some of the time and that's enough." Henry Kiser

---

17

"I always view problems as opportunities in work clothes." Henry Kiser

REVOLVING DEANSHIP

Ike Muslow, MD

$\mathcal{M}$y position as dean has been somewhat unusual in that I have served in this capacity on three occasions, all at the same institution. This service has spanned a time interval of twenty-two years, during ten of which I have been either dean or interim dean. My years in office were 1975 to 1981, 1990 to 1992, and 1996 to the present. Intervals between deanship were spent convalescing as vice chancellor for Shreveport affairs as a staff member for the chancellor.

Each tour has been distinctly different; the first was the most challenging and difficult. In 1975 we were a new school facing problems of accreditation, faculty recruitment, and limited budget. New schools at that time were not exactly appreciated by the old establishment. Problems were both external and internal. In 1975 there was plenty of space with little money; in 1990, no space and ample funds; in 1996, no space and no money. Given a choice, I would strongly recommend the dean choose money over space. There are many problems as well as opportunities associated with the deanship, but I shall review only three.

HOSPITAL-MEDICAL SCHOOL RELATIONSHIPS

Frequent discussions within the Council of Deans have revolved around the dean's role and responsibility for the major teaching hospital. Many have expressed the opinion that for the dean to be responsible also for hospital operations could drain the resources of the medical school and slant the decisions towards economic factors affecting the hospital.

I can consider it fortunate that one year into the deanship our medical school took over the ownership of a public hospital, its primary teaching institution. The dean was then CEO of the hospital. The two institutions were physically joined floor by floor, so distance was not a problem. The amalgamation went smoothly, probably because before being dean of the medical school, I had been director of the internal medicine department at the hospital and knew most of the employees. That personal bonding went a long way toward smoothing out any difficulties encountered. I encourage deans to rethink this issue rather than flee from that responsibility and opportunity. Academic hospital decisions must be based on the teaching role and patient care needs, and not solely on economic factors. It is necessary to recognize the tremendous difference in culture, and I would simply note that a hospital is opened 24 hours a day, 365 days a year. Contrast that to a medical school and you can appreciate the magnitude of the difference between institutions. Despite that, I believe it is important to have a single person responsible for both because it does not allow the faculty to play one administration against another.

MEDICAL SCHOOL ACCREDITATION

The accreditation process in the United States has done much to improve the quality of our medical school in terms of both environment and the education of our future physicians. Having said that, I would point out that pressures from the Liaison Committee for Medical Education and the Residency Review Committees can result in compromised decisions that ultimately are not in the best long-term interests of the institution or the educational programs. Building a quality faculty is never easy, but in the 1970s it was particularly difficult because of a shortage of surgical specialists and hospital-based physicians. New schools starting out, whether community-based schools, those with geographically separated campuses, or those attempting to follow the traditional model, were not always appreciated and supported by the old establishment. These external forces frequently used by internal groups to improve their own positions add enormously to the pressures faced by the dean. The ability to be a visionary and to look beyond the immediate demands of one pressure group over another is critical to the well-being of the dean, the deanship, and, ultimately, the institution and the people it serves.

DEPARTMENT CHAIRS

Ultimately, the department chairs are the critical ingredient in the selection and building of a faculty. They are the key to whatever can be accomplished in a deanship. Although all schools have search teams to find candidates to fill department chairs, it is the ultimate responsibility of the dean to make the final choice. My advice is, don't rush, know your institutional needs, use your fellow deans for recommendations, and do not let size of the CV make your decision. Most importantly, consider the person's personality and how that will fit into the culture of the institution as part of the selection criteria.

More difficult than filling a chair is removing one. Years ago at a deans' meeting, I was told that opportunities go in circles. So if the time is not right for a change, then wait, for you will get a second chance more favorable to you. Although a disruptive or ineffective chair must be removed, how and when that is done are most important. Having outside consultants review the department can be very helpful in providing support for your decision.

HONESTY AND HUMILITY

To be honest, I have told you more about deanship than I really know, but I have to summarize by saying, do not let the title make you think that you are more important than you really are. You will be surprised that, with all the publicity, few will recognize you outside your own institution, and many in your own institution will never have heard of you. Simply, do not be bothered by it. If you must spell your name for the operator, simply do it. Were it not rewarding, I would have never done it three times.

$\mathcal{T}$he art of getting along:

Sooner or later a dean, if he is wise, discovers that life is a mixture of good days and bad, victory and defeat, give and take.

He learns that it doesn't pay to be a sensitive sole—-that he should let some things go over his head like water off of a duck's back.

He learns that all men have burnt toast for breakfast now and then and that he shouldn't take the other fellow's grouch too seriously.

He learns that carrying a chip on his shoulder is the easiest way to get into a fight.

He learns that the quickest way to become unpopular is to carry tales and gossip about others.

He learns that it doesn't matter so much as who gets the credit so long as the organization prospers.

He learns that most of the other fellows are as ambitious as he is, that they have brains that are as good or better, and that hard work and not cleverness is the secret to success.

He learns buck passing always turns out to be a boomerang and that it never pays.

He comes to realize that the college could run perfectly well without him.

continued

He learns that even the janitor is human and that it doesn't do any harm to smile and say, 'good morning' even if it is raining.

He learns to sympathize with the youngsters coming into the organization because he remembers how bewildered he was when he first started out.

He learns that Presidents - Chancellors - Boards of Trustees are not monsters trying to get the last bit of work out of him for the least amount of pay but that usually they are fine people who have succeeded through hard work and who want to do the right thing.

He learns that the gang is not harder to get along with in one place than another and that 'getting along' depends about 98% on his own behavior.

(As modified from the writings of Wilfred A. Peterson)

18

> *"The measurable often drives out the important."*
>
> ~
>
> *"Far better an approximate answer to the right question which is often vague than an exact answer to the wrong question which can always be made precise."* TuKery

JOY AND DISAFFECTION DURING TWENTY-TWO YEARS AS A MEDICAL SCHOOL DEAN

John Naughton, MD

*T*he time required for cerebral downloading after an extended term as a medical school dean is longer than might be appreciated. Nevertheless, this publication permits the opportunity to initiate and organize the process so that a more comprehensive summation can be developed in some later years. For this paper, it should be sufficient to relate that I became dean at a relatively young age, 41, and was privileged to lead a medical school ready for change and success. Although the job posed challenges that others more qualified and experienced than I shunned, the opportunities presented coincided with my professional, intellectual, emotional, and personal commitments to medicine, medical education, biomedical research, and community service. I hope that a few reflections, as illustrated herein, can serve to inspire, not discourage, future leaders of academic medicine to aspire to serve in such an important position.

EXPERIENCES OF JOY

The rewards of my deanship were plentiful and bountiful. For me, HAPPINESS is represented by a few of the successes:
- building two large facilities, one dedicated to education, the other to biomedical research;
- securing a Robert Wood Johnson Generalist Physician Initiative, a Lucille B. Markey Research Center Designation, an NIH-sponsored Vanguard Women's Health Center Initiative, and a Positron Emission Tomography Center funded jointly by the Veterans Administration Health System and the SUNY system;
- graduating each year a class of medical students representative of the demography of New York State;
- participating in many educational innovations designed to improve the educational quality and effectiveness needed by students and GME trainees;
- developing a large, comprehensive, multi-institutional and multidisciplinary Graduate Medical Dental Education Consortium; and

• organizing and implementing a Faculty Practice Plan.

From my vantage point, these developments were achieved because of a faculty committed to the achievement of excellence and to the provision of leadership to students and institutional peers.

Each achievement obviously brought a degree of recognition and tremendous satisfaction. The attributes that I brought include a vision, commitment, the ability to negotiate, and a record of consistency, forthrightness, patience, and persistence. Somehow these characteristics were accepted by a faculty willing to take on the responsibility to bring each important task to successful completion.

DISAFFECTIONS

Fortunately, the joys outweighed the disappointments, but in every deanship, no matter how durable, there will be disaffections. For me, SADNESS is characterized as the following:
> • an inability to provide sufficient resources and support for every suggested worthwhile project - as resources diminish, the challenge is to say "no" consistently and graciously;
> • the inevitability that not every promising medical student or resident succeeds - it always seemed that for important decisions related to poor academic performance, the necessity to relay the decision to the involved medical student always fell on the dean's shoulders;
> • the loss of excellent faculty members to other worthy academic institutions;
> • the realization that the necessity for an organized faculty practice plan would strengthen the institution while simultaneously alienating many well-qualified, committed voluntary faculty members; and,
> • the failure of faculty leaders to expand their vision to include not only individual self-interests but also the broader needs of the school, patients, and the community.

It is easier to explore the reasons for success than to explore those for failure. The usual responses to a failed effort are expressed in terms such as a lack of available talent, too little time, inadequate resources, or recalcitrance. Perhaps an important lesson was to learn that within institutions not everyone can be expected to surrender deeply held values and beliefs to an overall institutional mission. As I reflect on those people who often were unable to participate in fostering change, I can see that it was because their views were diametrically different from those required to make a proposed initiative a success. Thus, one must prepare for failure by recognizing that differences between a dean and those he leads must not be personalized. Rather, everyone must appreciate the differences in values that must be shared if long-term substantial accomplishments are to be made.

PREPARATION

I was probably considered a "premature" dean. I recognize that for this job there is no standardized format for preparation. When I became dean, one of my closest friends was shocked that I left a viable, exciting, and productive academic career at an early age. Of course, he didn't envision the longevity that would transpire (neither did I!). Another well-known pediatric cardiologist actually scolded me about the career choice and declared that I had surrendered my independence. Certainly, that I had done in large part.

The important question should be, "How did I come to choose a job in which one is usually bound to fail?" I confess that it was a part of my career plan. The decision to enter academic medicine was made when I was a third-year medical student externing at the Lovelace Clinic in Albuquerque, New Mexico. It was there that I learned to integrate knowledge with patient care and to appreciate the excitement associated with teaching. Luckily, my mentors at Oklahoma recognized my commitment and potential, and each provided important support and advice. As a resident I had three mentors, each successful and yet quite diverse in individual interests and pursuits, who helped promote my research interests and development.

As my career unfolded, I positioned myself to become a professor and chairman of medicine. However, my research work covered several fields, and I quickly learned upon moving from Oklahoma City to Chicago that my interests would not be encompassed by a single discipline. Thus, my primary commitment would be to medical education and cardiac rehabilitation. The career development path was based solidly in internal medicine, cardiology, and physiology but expanded to include rehabilitation medicine and academic administration. In my view, the need today is for more academic leaders to be prepared in breadth as well as in depth. As I look back at such academic giants as Austin Flint, George Thorn, Sydney Farber, Fuller Albright, Alfred Fishman, and Albert Gelihorn, it seems that their depth was important to performance but their breadth was responsible for their creativity and multiple academic and social contributions.

THE DEAN AS LEADER

I charged many search committees over the years. Their members were often taken aback when I emphasized that leadership and management are not synonymous. They are not! A leader must have a philosophy, a vision, and a goal, which must be clearly and consistently enunciated to faculty members and students. Once enunciated, it must be adhered to in a consistent manner and altered only when additional knowledge and wisdom so dictate. One can lead an informed constituency but not a confused or indifferent one. In leading a faculty, I found it more important and productive to emphasize mission, goals, and values than those obstacles that can be used to justify inaction. Thus, leadership is needed to develop self-esteem and commitment is needed to achieve excellence. If a common set of goals can be developed, management will appropriately follow. Thus, leaders need not be technocratic, although managers must be.

*W*hen we realized it was your birthday, some of us reflected on what knowing you has meant. Others recalled special moments shared with you. And some became very quiet, and in their inner most feelings, thought to themselves, "Will there be cake?"

19

> *It is unreasonable to expect others to listen to your advice and ignore your example.*
>
> ~
>
> *Contentment is not the fulfillment of what you want, but the realization of what you already have.*

THE DEAN

Herbert Pardes, MD

I would never have guessed in my younger years that I would find myself in this position of reflecting on being a dean. I suspect that many people share the fantasy of playing center field for their favorite baseball team, but how many dream of being the dean of their favorite medical school?

The forces that bring one to such a position have much to do with both one's own personality and the needs of the institution that claims one. My understanding of how I arrived at this position goes something like this: I have always felt a need to try to solve the problems around me and to move toward the locus of authority that gives me the capacity to do that problem solving. Since my bailiwick is academic medicine, becoming dean was a reasonable outcome. School leadership decisions and policies have such profound effects on faculty members that it is natural for some of them to want to mold those decisions.

My grasp of the position of dean was limited when I started. I had no notion of the depths of the challenge already there as I assumed the position, challenges destined to increase with the changes in health care and the nationwide focus on reducing budgets.

MOVING IMMOVABLE OBJECTS

Being a dean has been full of gratifications, including working with countless outstanding people (students, faculty members, staff, alumni, etc.), promoting quality and innovative teaching, generating a sense of enthusiasm and vigor, building a much improved physical plant, recruiting and retaining good faculty, strengthening finances, and relating the center to industry, to community, to government. Whether pressing for productive health policy or finding dollars for a medical student learning center, there are goals to be determined, strategies to be found, immovable objects to be moved, and excellence to be achieved.

IF WE DO NOT HAVE SOME FAILURE—
WE ARE NOT TRYING HARD ENOUGH

There have also been failures: people whom we could not retain, people whom we could not attract, grant applications that were not successful, fund raising efforts that did not work, and obstacles that just would not budge.

When I ask why we did not succeed in some of the efforts we attempted, I conclude that if we do not have some failures, we are not trying hard enough. To make this enterprise work, you have to take risks, you need to exhaust every conceivable opportunity. The needs are great because of the constant demand of a medical school for resources and the inherently expensive nature of the enterprise.

> *A mistake is proof that someone at least tried to accomplish something.*

INDIVIDUAL ISSUES NOT TRIVIAL

While doing this—i.e., running a multi-million-dollar enter-prise—the dean must meet extraordinary interpersonal challenges. Deans have to accommodate a very large number of individuals and groups. Faculty members and students are not a homogeneous society. Individual complaints, desires, and concerns are omnipresent. When the air conditioning goes out in laboratories and critical experiments are threatened, when housing is hard to get for young students and faculty members, when a position is needed for a spouse in recruiting a person from another part of the country, deans and their staffs become involved in a welter of individual issues that must not be treated as trivial .

Beyond these types of issues, however, are the inevitable ten-sions, conflicts, and concerns about needs for space, money, renova-tions, personnel changes, and housing assistance. These require the skills of a mentor, negotiator, psychiatrist, advocate, lawyer, minister, marriage counselor, etc. As you might say in New York, "You need a Mensch."

I can not stress enough the need to be sensitive to an enormous diversity of constituencies—basic science and clinical faculty members, students and teachers, research leaders and junior investigators, alumni and current students, administrative staff and faculty, people in other parts of the University and people in the medical center, hospital people, donors and trustees.

Most important, in all of this, is the need to try to understand and attend to the individual concern, the individual need for recognition, appreciation, understanding, confidence, and support.

SPECIAL FEELINGS

There are times of great humor—like when a faculty member shows the dean how the dean can solve many problems by giving that faculty member the space of others, or when during a faculty meeting discussing for the first time a dean's tax, one of the faculty members asks whether this is done at any other medical schools in this country. There are also times of special feeling, such as when clinical faculty leaders have the privilege and extraordinary pleasure of awarding medical school diplomas to their own children, or when the entire university assemblage listens during the university graduation to the words of the Hippocratic Oath meant particularly for the physicians who are graduating, but in many ways applicable to the entire assemblage.

WORDS OF ADVICE

To ask how I might approach the job of dean if I started over makes me wonder how much more I know than I did before. I am not sure in how many instances I would have done things dramatically differently from what I have done.

In reflecting on that, however, I felt it might be valuable to pass on some words of advice more systematically. A list of suggestions, some of which may be applicable more broadly than to just deaning, is offered in no particular order:

• Be true to your word. Nothing is more critical than your credibity. If a person (or aninstitution) develops the reputation he will not do what he says that he will do for faculty members or other people with whom he interacts, the person(or institution) loses a most important asset.

• Promulgate a set of goals or principles. For example,
    The patient is the first priority.
    Pursue excellence in all activities of the medical school.
    Encourage open and honest discussion of the
        important issues.
    Value and promote the advance of knowledge.

• Deans should reflect those values that they have chosen in every action, word, or communication. In the end, the most cherished aspect of a medical school is that it stands for a universally lauable mission. This is important for others to know. It is also important for deans and their staffs to keep this in mind, because it should help them feel good about the many mundane things they have to do in the service of a higher mission.

• Be even-handed in response to faculty members and departments. That is not to say that there are not times when a department may have a particularly important mission that justifies the school's making a decision to strengthen dramatically its work in cancer or in cardiovascular disease, or for children or for women. But beyond those points of emphasis, all faculty members are valued, and all departments are important to the mission of the medical school.

• The dean should be courageous and stand up against myopia, prejudice, and single-issue zealots. There are unfortunately people who are excessively aggressive in pushing for anti-abortion policies, for anti-animal research policies, for anti-genetic research policies. I have received considerable criticism from such groups, including one that attacked Columbia's decision to focus on complementary medicine. Although the dean should be open to and respectful of opposing positions, intimidation of faculty or distortion of curriculum or research on the part of narrow-minded or anti-intellectual forces should be resisted. A scientist attacked by anti-animal research groups should be supported and protected, assuming that he or she is abiding by appropriate standards for animal care and does research that is not frivolous.

• Celebrate the diversity of your faculty, staff and student body. All people must be respected. Do not assume that because you believe you are open-minded, everyone else in the institution is as sensitive as they should be. It is an important goal that the medical profession incorporate all cultures an backgrounds so that the marvelous nature of this country is fully realized. When the profession does this, all patients are afforded the option of securing care from people who uniquely understand and resonate to their cultures and backgrounds.

• Restrain your anger and avoid actions that seem driven by or overly influenced by a sense of annoyance, irritation, or fury. You may make the same decision later, but I have never found it helped me when I acted impulsively from a feeling of such anger. People at times say and do silly things. Reports of their actions or statements are often distorted. Make sure you have the facts, make sure you have all the various accounts, and then, after adequate breathing space, make your decision in a more serene and rational fashion.

• Maintain an office with accessibility. Be open to input from everyone. The dean's office should not be seen as some remote, rarified enterprise housing strange, unfamiliar, and exotic people. The fact that you listen does not mean that you have to act. As a confidante retain the confidence that you promise. The belief and realization that the dean is a sensible person to whom one can speak enhances the sense of closeness to leadership, fosters a better feeling about the school, and encourages a sense of solidarity with the school.

• Value people of the academic center at all levels of the organization. All are making some contribution to the academic health center. The administrator who makes sure the grant gets out and in appropriate form, the facilities manager who responds to the emergency, the student aid counselor who responds to students in a thoughtful and sensitive way, the development staff who try to accommodate the diverse needs both of the faculty and the potential donors, these along with many others make the institution go forward. The star clinicians, scientists, educators, and students make a school's reputation but are insufficient to make it run.

• Be active politically. The medical school is influenced by decisions at every level of government. We are well past the days when we could sit back and assume that the world would take care of the medical school. The dean should make the case regarding the fragile funding of medical schools. If the money isn't there, the minority students, the young researcher, and the outstanding leaders in education, clinical work, and research will not be supported. The very basis for our nation's distinction in medical research and medical care will be seriously undermined. Fight for the things that will strengthen the institution.

• Learn how to raise funds. It is an intimate part of the general function and tone of the school. Success in fund raising can foster morale, pride in the school's programs and people, and participation by all the constituencies in a sense of ownership of the school.

• Conduct yourself with dignity, because you stand for the school and for the values of academics and medicine as well as leadership in society. Unfortunately, the number of leaders in society and certainly the number who are respected are few. Medicine, universities, science, and other helping professions are all functions or services that deserve respect and support. One of the benefits of being a dean is that you stand for them.

• Play a role in the university and with your fellow deans and faculty members. The medical school has a special character, and yet it is only one part of the university. Running a university today is an enormously formidable undertaking. The medical school that functions as contributor and concerned party working with other academic leaders is valued by others and should be reciprocal. In turn they will be more supportive of the medical school's special needs.

• Enjoy the successes of the students and faculty. Tell them when you are pleased with what they have done. I write when I receive word of a patient well cared for, a student having done well, a noteworthy achievement by one of the faculty members in science or in education or in the community, etc. You are the leader: you speak for the institution in communicating your pleasure, and pride in the given person is invaluable to the recipient of that communication.

• Foster a sense of tolerance, generosity, and understanding of human weakness while asserting high standards. None of us is perfect; we can only strive to be as good as possible. Flexibility and understanding should not be confused with weakness or taken to mean that you condone mediocrity. A certain humility and understanding of the pressures on people is vital in the complex of human affairs with which the dean and the team in the dean's office will contend.

At the end of the day, the dean can feel pleasure and pride when the faculty members make sure that patients are well treated and sometimes saved; when students exit the medical school as outstanding, caring young physicians who will make contributions to medicine and their society; when a gene is discovered, a new surgical technique developed, a virus identified, by scientists at your institution; and when the multitude of mothers, fathers, children, and other relatives share your pleasure in the White Coat Ceremony or at the graduation of those very valued new young physicians .

Being a dean is not easy, but when you think of the missions you are advancing, it is a life and role of incalculable consequence for society and for your fellow human beings.

By working faithfully eight hours a day, you may eventually get to be a dean and work 12 hours a day.

20

> *T*he best executive is the one
> who has sense enough to pick good men
> to do what needs to be done,
> and the self restraint to keep from meddling
> with them while they do it.

REFLECTIONS OF A DEAN

Robert G. Petersdorf, MD

I have been watching deans, thinking about what they do and how they do it, for nearly twenty-five years. My first point of observation was as a chairman of a department of medicine where I served under two deans and one interim dean. My second viewpoint was as a hospital CEO in a private medical school, a position in which I did not report to the dean. Then I thought I should try deaning myself and spent five years as dean, during most of which I was also vice chancellor for health affairs. And finally, during the last eight years of my career, when I was president of the Association of American Medical Colleges (AAMC), I worked for no fewer than 125 deans. Although the AAMC has multiple constituencies, the deans are the most influential. Not too long ago, the AAMC was strictly a deans' club, and sometimes the deans still consider themselves the hub of the association. Certainly those of us on the staff of the AAMC tried hard to keep the deans happy, and when they were happy, so was the staff. The reverse was also true.

I summarized the subject of deans and deaning in a changing world in the first Robert Ebert Memorial Lecture in April of 1997[†]. In this talk, I analyzed the demography of deans, the causes of decanal unhappiness, the changing external environment, the medical schools' agendas, and tips for deanly survival, both professional and personal. I do not wish to repeat what I said in that paper, but I do want to expand on the overlying theme of the dean's broad-based constituency. A good deal of this essay will be autobiographical, and little of it is data-driven.

THE DEAN'S DIVERSIFIED CONSTITUENCY

Most of the important tasks that a dean performs deal with people. Although there are different reporting relationships, I want to use as the model for this discussion the dean/CEO (I was called dean/vice chancellor). In that situation, reporting to the dean are the medical school, the practice plan, and those teaching hospitals that are owned or managed by the university. In this type of set-up, the other health science schools usually do not report to the dean of medicine;

they tend to report to the provost.

THE DEAN-HOSPITAL DIRECTOR INTERACTION

The first lesson that deans must learn, even when they are the CEO, is that they do not really know how to run hospitals. I came to the position of hospital CEO from a chairmanship of medicine, and I must confess, in retrospect, that I had to learn a lot about running a hospital, and most deans are no exception. It is extremely important, therefore, for a dean/CEO not to micromanage. The dean must also understand that the hospital director has to have one eye on the bottom line. There is nothing that makes hospital directors (or university presidents) more nervous than to have the hospital operating in the red. At the same time, the dean has to make sure that the hospital director keeps an eye on the academic ball. This is not always easy. It requires that the hospital director maintain a balance between the hospital's productivity and the academic programs. The external environment has brought deans and hospital directors closer together. After all, deans have to have their troops - the faculty members - march at a faster pace, and hospital directors need to make their institutions more user-friendly. Deans and hospital directors usually come from very different backgrounds. Like most people, they have sizable egos, and they must avoid petty jealousies. One of the most abrasive surfaces is their comparative salaries. Both should be paid well, and neither should be paid excessively. Often, there is little chemistry between them, and they have to try to manufacture a chemical reaction that makes them compatible.

DEANS AND CHAIRS

A successful medical school needs a group of chairs that share the institution's mission with the dean. This is particularly true for the clinical agenda. I recall an incident when I was dean that led to conflict between me and the chair of medicine. As dean, I was constantly bombarded with complaints about the clinical reluctance of the department of medicine. The faculty members in the department were concerned primarily with research and did as little clinical work as they could get away with. After gathering data on the department of medicine's lack of clinical productivity, I confronted the chair. I was told in no uncertain terms that the chair and I were on different wave lengths. The department of medicine recruited its faculty members for their ability to obtain research grants, not because of their clinical expertise. I was told that if new faculty members in the department were clinically-competent, it was a pleasant but totally unrequired bonus. Research and obtaining research grants were the name of the game. The interchange occurred at a time when there was a good deal of pressure on the institution to increase its clinical activities. The hospital needed to fill its beds; the students and house staff needed patients from whom they could learn; and faculty members needed more clinical income if they were to be paid. It was my experience that surgeons were generally more likely to be clinically effective - maybe they needed to work harder to earn their generally higher salaries - and departments of medicine were less likely to put out the same degree of clinical effort. Pediatrics and OB were somewhere in between, and both of those departments were less likely to attract paying patients than did departments of medicine or surgery.

Clinical departments have become very large. They are much more dependent on clinical income than ever before. This fact requires some management skills on the part of clinical department chairs. When I first became a department chair, the department never made much clinical income, in part because the faculty members did not document their services well. However, in these days of clinician/teachers who just about have to earn their own way, clinical productivity is at a premium, and the chair has to place more emphasis on it than was the case in the past. Chairs should ultimately be held responsible for keeping their departments on a fiscally even keel. There are only two reasons for clinical departments to lose money: either the department is too large or the salaries of the faculty members are too high. Departments of pediatrics and OB might be the exception to this rule. If a department of medicine really wants to be a research-oriented department, it must put part of the faculty members' salaries on research grants. It can no longer count on busy clinicians to subsidize their more research-oriented colleagues. I know of departments of medicine that lose a million dollars a year, year in and year out. There is no excuse for that. Those departments require restructuring. There are, regrettably, also departments of surgery that are losing a significant amount of money. There is even less excuse for them than for departments of medicine. Departments of surgery tend to be smaller and, when they lose money, their faculty members are usually paid too much.

I firmly believe that department chairs and, for that matter, deans should be reviewed every five to six years and, if their management skills are found wanting, they should be replaced. Routine reviews do away with unexpected and usually traumatic firings. Where such reviews have become part of the academic process, they have greatly enhanced academic accountability.

DEANS AND VICE PRESIDENTS

Many people have written about the frequently abrasive interface between the dean of the school of medicine and the vice president for health affairs. Because the model of dean I have chosen also makes the dean vice president for medical affairs, I will not discuss in this essay the situation in which the dean reports to the vice president. As for the relationship between the dean of the medical school and other health science schools, a reporting relationship where all of those deans report to a single vice president raises uncomfortable questions of equity, which can be avoided if the dean of the school of medicine has a different reporting relationship than do the deans of other health science schools.

THE DEAN'S TEAM

Some deans like to operate with a deputy dean who functions as the dean's alter ego. Sometimes this works and sometimes it doesn't. Deans who opt for this management model certainly have to choose deputy deans who share their vision, goals, and management style.

I have preferred at least two very strong senior associate deans - one for academic affairs and the other for administration. Many of the dean's duties can be transferred to these associate deans. If they are tough-minded negotiators, they can be very helpful to the dean, particularly in working out recruitment packages with new chairs. They often have much more detailed knowledge of the resources available and of the status of the department to which new chairs are being recruited. This is particularly true if the chair being recruited wants to bring a "group." I recall an unfortunate incident in which an incoming chair brought virtually an entirely new department, and all the division heads that were in place had to be replaced. Some of the incumbents did not take that kindly and dropped lawsuits on the incoming chair. This entire mess could have been avoided if more time had been taken during the recruitment negotiations and if the dean had delegated responsibility for some of the details to strong associate deans. I recall another example in which the dean, unfamiliar with the details of what was going on in the hospital, committed the same set of beds to two new chairs, a totally avoidable imbroglio. Although strong academic affairs and administrative associate deans might function as premium inter pares, a successful dean's team requires associate deans (some call them medical directors and some vice presidents for medical affairs) at each of the large affiliated hospitals. This is particularly true in today's environment, when the hospitals might be affiliated for academic purposes but be deadly competitors for patients and clinical programs.

Last, but by no means least, the practice plan director (who in many instances is also the dean's representative for managed care) is playing a progressively important role. Such a person is essential for ensuring that the hospital, the faculty members, and the entire clinical operation stay in step.

DEANS AND MEDICAL STUDENTS

One would think that the education of students is the primary raison d'etre for the dean's existence and that deans must spend a
good deal of time and effort in this arena. Alas, such is seldom the
case. Even when I was dean, in the early 1980s, the only time that I
saw medical students was when one of them was in trouble and faced
probation, expulsion, or some other punitive measure. The other
times when I saw medical students were at the opening convocation
and at commencement. Of course, because the dean sponsored a
monthly science lecture followed by a reception, he could mingle with
medical students who were always at these lectures in profusion - I
think more in order to eat than to learn. There are, of course, exceptions. There are deans who entertain small groups of medical students
in their homes, a most admirable practice. The late dean at the
University of Washington sponsored students who had done research
at the regional research meetings in Carmel. He also attended almost
all of the student presentations and then gave a dinner for the students. These actions led to a sense of camaraderie between the dean
and the students even though they did not see one another the rest of
the year. But such actions are distinctly unusual. I recall that when I
did research as a third- and fourth-year medical student at Yale, an
institution that required a thesis, we had no contact with the dean and
certainly no sponsorship at meetings or free dinners.

DEANS, ALUMNI, AND SUPPORT GROUPS

The school at which I was dean was very young. In fact, it cel-
ebrated the tenth anniversary of its first graduating class on my watch.
It therefore did not have much of an alumni body. I must say that my
own alma mater is much more solicitous of its alumni than was the
institution at which I was dean. I suspect that most of this relationship is based on the need for the school to get the alumni to open their
wallets. I have no quarrel with that, particularly since most alumni are
fortunate to have made a very good living. Because we have educated

our own children (or in some instances grandchildren), I can think of few other causes as worthy as giving to one's medical alma mater.

When I was dean we were fortunate to have some support groups who had taken the medical school on as a cause. I had not been familiar with this phenomenon and, when I first became dean, I paid little attention to these support groups. I had this matter called to my attention by my chancellor (to whom the leaders of the support group had complained), and I rectified my error by hiring a retired surgeon from the community to function as associate dean for community affairs. It turned out to be a brilliant stroke because the associate dean put together a street fair that earned a sizable amount of money for various academic enterprises and that is still in existence some 15 years later.

DEANS AND THE VETERANS ADMINISTRATION

A significant number of medical schools have affiliations with the Veterans Administration, which, by definition, makes the dean the chair of a dean's committee. I would urge deans to take this obligation seriously. Although medical schools often help the VA to fulfill its academic mission, the VA hospitals constitute a significant venue for teaching medical students, residents, and other health professionals whose education is under the aegis of the medical school. The VA is undergoing significant reorganization into twenty-two integrated service networks. This reorganization has placed considerable stress on the medical school and its VA hospital partner. It is important to keep this alliance productive.

DEANS AND PRESIDENTS OR PROVOSTS

Deans of medical schools and presidents and provosts to whom the deans often report come from very different backgrounds. Both the medical school dean and the university officials often have very steep learning curves to be able to understand one another. I have found that keeping the lines of communication open is extremely important. University presidents (and provosts) don't like surprises, particularly in the form of red ink at the medical school and its teaching hospitals. One of the best ways to keep these people supportive is for them to receive their clinical care at the academic medical center. Personal interest by the medical faculty who have university officials as patients leads to a much higher level of interest and support from these people.

DEANS AND FACULTY MEMBERS

I have never been a fan of faculty governance. Academic medicine is fundamentally a hierarchical system in which deans, department chairs, division heads, and others govern the faculty. This leaves the faculty members to do the things that they should be able to do best - teach, do research, and tend to patient care (where appropriate). Most medical schools have large administrative staffs, and these people must be permitted to do their jobs without debating the medical school's multiple issues at endless faculty meetings. This does not mean that I would contest the faculty's traditional privileges over admissions, standards of student performance, or curriculum. Likewise, faculty members need to be consulted, particularly about changes that affect them. However, for the most part, such changes do not need to be put to a vote of the entire faculty to be implemented. I know of institutions at which the faculty members quite literally vote on what day of the week it is. I remain to be convinced that those institutions teach better, make more and better discoveries, and take better care of patients.

CONCLUDING REMARKS

I hope that this brief essay has presented evidence that the dean has a diverse constituency, each member of which has higher expectations of the dean than the dean can deliver. However, by learning to delegate and by communicating freely and frequently (face to face as often as possible and not entirely by email), deans will enjoy what they do. I found deaning to be a constant challenge. Although it may be argued that I was a dean in more tranquil times, it didn't seem so at the time. I would also urge present and future deans to limit the time that they are in the deanship. Ten or fifteen years would seem to be enough for anyone. There are plenty of us around who have enjoyed productive lives after deaning, and I hope that today's deanery learns from those of us who have "been there and done that."

REFERENCES

[1]Petersdorf, R.G. "Deans and Deaning in a Changing World." *Academic Medicine,* 1997, 72:953-958.

*T*he controversial dean asked his secretary, "Why is it that people take an instant dislike to me?" The secretary replied, "It saves them time."

21

> *O*ften times we change not when we see
> the light but when we feel the heat.

MEDICAL DEANING IN THE
LATTER HALF
OF THE 20th CENTURY

James A. Pittman, Jr., MD

$\mathcal{B}$eing dean of a medical school in the latter half of this century has been great. It was a time of explosive increases in money poured into health care from federal programs like Medicare and Medicaid in 1965; unprecedented growth in construction of facilities for hospitals, medical schools, and laboratories; and most of all exciting post-war accomplishments in research, beginning with the wartime leadership of Vannevar Bush[1]. The support of the NIH, led by physician's son Senator Lister Hill, expanded from a few million dollars in 1948 to a total of some $15 billion dollars by the end of the century. This plus the billions from industry and private sources resulted in the development of a multitude of antibiotics, new technologies, DNA's double helix structure in 1953, further spectacular advances in our understanding of gene structure, and now the human genome project and the prospect of gene therapy. Teaching also exploded, with an approximate doubling of medical student enrollment and the number of medical schools between 1950 and 1982[2].

THE JOB OF DEAN

What were the important aspects of being dean of a medical school during those times? How could a dean of medicine take advantage of those opportunities and help the school to undertake important improvements? Are those characteristics important for the future?

The job is changing, like everything else, as the dean of medicine becomes progressively more submerged in hierarchy and embedded in sclerotic bureaucracies just when the environment of medicine is transforming as rapidly as clouds in a summer thunderstorm. My belief is that medicine in general (that is, care of sick and potentially sick people) will prosper only if some balance can be found between uncontrolled arrogant, arbitrary, and greedy dictatorship of MDs on the one hand and their submersion in a pseudodemocratic politically based commercialism on the other. Thus, the dean of medicine (an MD[a]) of the future should be <u>also</u> the provost, vice president, and vice

[a] Very few Ph.D.s served as medical school deans during the latter half of the century. Len Napolitano of New Mexico, Ernst Knobil of U. Texas/Houston, and Charles Baugh of U. South Alabama come to mind as three of the most prominent. Although these were successful deans, if one is training people to practice medicine, it is probably best to have a dean who has been through that training. Otherwise, a hospital administrator or other lay manager might do as well.

chancellor for health affairs (over medical school personnel, finances, space, etc., as well as hospital, practice plan, and research activities) and for the education of other members of the health care team. The main point is that the dean of medicine, whatever the title, should <u>also</u> oversee all of the other health-professional schools (nursing, dentistry, allied health, public health, pharmacy, optometry, etc.). This belief is certainly politically incorrect, offensive to the non-M.D. health professionals, and unlikely to come about soon if ever in any universal way, but it will, in any case, be part of the ever-developing system of health care in the United States and the world. These beliefs and suggestions are based on the ideas that some sort of hierarchical structure is inevitable in healthcare. People don't really want their health cared for. Rather, they want help when they don't feel well, although sometimes they do want help to try to avoid getting sick (vaccinations, advice on diets and exercise, etc).[3] The person most highly educated, knowledgeable, and skilled in that discipline <u>should</u> be the physician, and thus the physician should be the leader of the team - an inflammatory phrase to the nurse practitioners (who during the 1970s and 1980s rode the crest of feminism, only to be cut short by events such as more male nurses, but who remain aggressive as the millennium ends), turf-accumulating optometrists, and pharmacists (whose schools <u>all</u> upgraded from giving BS degrees to granting doctoral degrees during the latter half of this century to join the osteopaths and chiropractors), etc.[b] In this inevitable hierarchy, form should follow function, and skill, demonstrated knowledge, and helpful attitudes should be determinative, not power politics. An unattainable utopia, perhaps, but still worth striving for.

<u>Priorities</u>

People

The most important thing is the <u>people</u>. If one has good people, the school and its products will be good. Which people? Is it more

---

[b] Nowadays almost every self-respecting human being is "a doctor." Lawyers are Doctors of Jurisprudence (the JD degree given by law schools in the U.S.), and even Fidel Castro is known as "Doctor Castro." See what I mean?

important to have excellent students or excellent faculty members? Obviously, it is best to have both. Excellent faculty members will demand high standards for performance and accomplishment from the students. However, excellent students will demand excellent faculty members. Because the composition of the student body is more subject to circumstances external to the school and the dean's control, it is probably best for the dean to try first for excellent faculty members, while not neglecting pursuit of the most excellent students.

How does one determine "excellence" in a faculty member or a person? It is a closed conservative system. To find an expert in subject X, one asks other experts in subject X. They say, "Joe Doaks of San Francisco is among the best in the world, maybe the very best, in subject X." The dean knows nearly nothing about subject X (but not quite nothing). So he trusts the assessments of acknowledged experts (acknowledged, of course, by other experts). Science and medicine are conservative, slow-changing, cautious, careful disciplines. Wild outliers among potential recruits may be the very best, but they come with very high risk and often turn out to be costly failures.

How, then, does the dean of medicine identify and recruit excellent faculty members? The traditional way is to form a search committee of concerned persons - often termed "stake holders." This is now a political necessity.[c] Candidates from the dean's own institution should almost always be on the list (but usually not on the search committee), and internal appointments have many advantages. But external candidates should never be excluded. A search committee does not preclude the dean from carrying out his own search or from guiding the search process.[d] People who apply for a job are usually not

---

[c] On the other hand, when I nominated a friend (who very much wanted the job and was a reasonable candidate in everybody's mind) for Dean of Medicine at Harvard, with the request to President Bok that he pass this nomination and CV on to "the appropriate committee," I received the response that "there was no search committee; that is not Harvard's way." In other words, the President would nose around and ask opinions, then name the dean himself. Not a bad system.

[d] Rudi Schmid, Dean of Medicine at UCSF, was a great dean in my estimation. He fearlessly made his own decisions on the basis of his own judgements. When the search committee for chief of surgery handed in a conservative list of "leading surgeons of the nation," he tossed it in the trash and appointed Haile Debasse, who wasn't even on the list but was so successful he was later made Dean of Medicine following Schmid.

the best choices. The best candidates are usually those happy where they are, perhaps ready to move but not desperate to move. It is critical that the dean himself call people he knows to obtain information as accurate as possible. It is worthless to ask, or worse to write, people the dean does not know at all and request such sensitive information. If possible, it is advisable for the dean to travel to the institutions of the final few candidates and interview as many people as possible at all levels to gain that kind of information. In a few instances, several members of the search committee have traveled to the final candidate's school to interview the candidate's colleagues.

What does one look for? As mentioned above, it is something of a closed system. One asks other leaders in the same field (medicine, surgery, biochemistry, etc.) whether this person is very highly regarded in that field of endeavor. Is the candidate productive and expert in the three traditional areas of patient care, teaching, and research (in that order for the clinical disciplines; reverse order for the more scientific)? Whether the candidate will be a good administrator is often more difficult to discern, especially in the case of research where a very productive investigator may have had little administrative experience beyond his own lab. The question hinges largely on what kind of person the candidate is. Does the candidate get along well with colleagues, or is he chronically hyper-aggressive, dictatorial, and predatory? Some "difficult" people are the best in their fields, and they may be a great catch for a dean. However, they need to be placed in situations where the negative aspects of their personalities do not precipitate repeated confrontations and crises.

Is the candidate a good mentor? That is, does the candidate take a personal interest in guiding and promoting students, post-docs, and others in their careers, or is the candidate a selfish people-user? I used to try to assess a "Generosity Index" for potential recruits. W.R. Brinkley, PhD,[e] for example, is not only a great cell biologist, but also has a maximum Generosity Index and supports and cooperates readily with others, without being naively taken over by aggressors. In any case, the dean's perceptiveness and aggressiveness in assessing these

[e] Brinkley was Chairman of Cell Biology and Anatomy at UAB and is now Vice President and Dean of the Graduate School at Baylor University.

things will go far in determining success in recruiting top faculty members.

As just mentioned, one should not rule out all "difficult people" as faculty members, or some medical stars will be missed. However, an institution constantly riven by faculty fights and office politics is in trouble, and one characterized by harmonious, smooth-running teamwork is likely to prosper. It is the <u>people</u> involved who will make the difference, not only the organizational arrangements and resources[f]. And, finally, if the dean really <u>likes</u> the individual faculty members, respects them, and finds interacting with them pleasant and intellectually stimulating, things are likely to go well. You can't really fake these things. On the other hand, you can make a conscious effort to see the other person' s point of view sympathetically. Failure to do that tends to precipitate confrontations. The dean should also get out on the front lines as much as possible, visiting attending physicians and students on rounds, visiting labs during the day, talking with people about what they are doing, eating lunch frequently with students and faculty members (separately), and meeting with faculty members in <u>their</u> offices rather than his own. That provides the added advantage of being able to leave and terminate the meeting more easily than having to kick them out of your own office. A dean who sits in his office hunched over his computer all day looking at dollars and space is not long for this job. But there is another less readily resolvable conflict here. Schools want their leaders to be "major national or international leaders," which requires that the Dean spend lots of time on the road, which interferes with doing the job at home. Answer: Work harder!

Students

The same qualities for excellence are sought in students, but

---

[f] There are, however, situations in which the organizational structure is largely determinative. One of the best memoranda I ever wrote was known in my office as "the cockroach memo." Several respected senior faculty members were complaining that "the Dean is wasting time and muddying the waters by fiddling with organization." I responded that a cockroach, immediately after it has been swatted and killed, retained exactly the same components as a few moments before: same wings, antennae, legs, even the same molecules. The only thing changed was the organization. I thought that was a great memo.

no school should be limited to a single geographic area, such as a state. State legislatures[g] do not want to support a school with 100% "foreigners," but a few out-of-state and out-of-U.S. students, if really good, add tremendously to a student body and to the level of scholarship and learning.

Balance

Patient care, teaching, and research must be balanced. Faculty members who are clinically active must be really superb and "exemplary" (how else to teach) in clinical medicine in their disciplines. They should do scholarly work, but their devotion to patient care and their clinical skills must not wither from neglect. They must take an active, sympathetic, and supportive role in the clinical affairs of their colleagues, not stay in the laboratory or on the road all the time with little regard for day-to-day clinical activities.[h]

Research is required of all faculty members, but it need not always be laboratory based and grant supported, although a medical school without a large component of this type of research tends to be intellectually stagnant and marginal. If clinicians do no research at all (including multiple scholarly case reports or series, outcomes research, epidemiology, etc.), they might be better off in private practice, and the school might also be better off.

Teaching, unfortunately, usually comes out last. However, teaching is not the most important thing in education; <u>learning</u> is. Great teachers, such as Tinsley R. Harrison of **Harrison's Principles of Internal Medicine** text, are essential for a school. This is also a complex subject, but if the clinical practice and research to which the students are exposed are superb, and if the students are bright and inquisitive, they are likely to learn.

---

[g] Usually it is not the abstract idealism of "servicing my state" that precipitates these problems, but rather the fact that some legislator's nephew did not get into medical school.

[h] Eugene Stead, the famous Chief of Medicine at Duke, said that the first thing he wanted to see when recruiting a division chief was the person's travel schedule, which, with small subterfuges, he could obtain from the recruitee's secretary ("Send me a copy of his schedule for the next six months so we can arrange a trip.") If he was scheduled to be mostly out of town, he was eliminated.

STANDARDS

Some degree of elitism is inevitable in a technologic society such as ours. Extreme free-marketers, such as Milton Friedman (who opposes licensure and even registration of specialists and favors fee commercial combat[4]), are not correct and are unlikely to prevail. Who wants to choose an airline on the basis of an unregulated advertisement of this particular pilot's expertise? Credentials are inevitable, and they should reflect real standards. In other words, they should be honest and accurate. Here again we are trapped to a large degree in a conservative system of experts, but we must not fight it too vigorously for fear of ossification. Rather, we must insist on maintenance of purposeful standards of performance and accomplishment in scientific medicine. If you can't pass the tests, you can't get an M.D. degree from this medical school. Sorry.

FACILITIES, MONEY, ENDOWMENT

Facilities, money, and endowments are absolutely essential, and the more there are, the better the medical school is likely to be. But they must not dominate everything. Some schools have good facilities and large amounts of state support yet still seem unable to achieve excellence. However, if the faculty members and students are superb and have some voice in administrative matters, they will help with the money and facilities and keep the academic standards high and patients are more likely to receive optimal medical care than otherwise.

Internal management and constraints are frequently more important than external (e.g., a state legislature). In distribution of space I used to make "space rounds" between 2:00 and 4:00 AM. During the day, "space rounds" sometimes precipitated fits of hysteria among nervous faculty members, so I went at night. I always took with me (1) a security officer (policeman) so that I could gain access to any room and to make sure that I could not be accused of stealing something, and (2) a Polaroid camera to record (with room number visible if possible) the furniture stacked in the lab the chief claimed was in "constant heavy research use" but was in reality a store room (Interestingly, the only people working in those labs at 3:00 AM were Orientals).

ADMINISTRATIVE SERVICE

Deans who view their job as "Director and CEO of the Company" may, if they last and have high academic standards, get a good medical school (although it may look more like a docile army than a gathering of collegial scholars). But the most successful deans of medicine are those who are shrewd enough to leave a high scholarly imprint on the institution without trying to order people around. That is, those who view themselves as part of the supporting infrastructure that makes the scholarly activity possible. Such deans serve the faculty members and students. The best dean is one who "carries the water" for the faculty members. Here we come to the greatest Dean of all time: Gunga Dean.

> You may talk of gin and beer,
> When you're sent to teaching rounds and lab-space shot it;
> But when it come to patient care,
> Don't leave SERVICE, don't you dare!
> Or you'll lick the bloomin' boots of 'im that's got it
> Oh, it's Dean, Dean, Dean — (ad paradisium).

REFERENCES

1. Zachary, G. P., *Endless Frontier: Vannevar Bushy Engineer of the American Century.* New York, Free Press, 1997.

2. AAMC data (available on internet):
The number of medical school first-year enrollees (slightly higher than new entrants, because of recycled first-year students) was 7,177 in 1950 and had almost doubled to 14,763 by 1974. It peaked in 1981 at 17,200 and has remained around that number since. The number of schools is more complex, due to the change from two-year to four-year schools during the 1950s and '60s, as well as founding of completely new schools. The number was about 86 in 1960 (Dr. Paul Jolly, AAMC) and peaked at 127 in 1981 (with the

founding of Mercer), and now has fallen slightly to 124 at the end of the 1990s.

3. Pittman, J.A. "Health Care, Medical Cost Accounting, and the GNP." **J. Med. Assn. State of Alabama, 1978.**

4. Friedman, M. **Capitalism and Freedom**. Chicago, University of Chicago Press, 1962.

*T*his story is told about a meeting of the Harvard Overseers when they were asked to review the goals of the medical school, some 26 worthy goals. The then Chairman of Monsanto spoke up and said, "Well I'm only a soap salesman, but if you want to accomplish anything worthwhile, select three or four and achieve them."

22

> *T*hose who complain about the way a ball bounces
> are usually the ones who dropped it.

SOME THOUGHTS
ON DEANING

Perry Rigby, MD

$\mathcal{T}$he day the dean begins is the end of a cumulative process and initiates the sentence to live in day-tight compartments. The new dean has won the job; credentials, values and virtues are in order; expectations are high; and it is on-the-job training from now on.

He sets about discovering what is inherited and acquired, learning the sum of institutional history and its people and materials, and proceeds to work to overcome obstacles, solve problems, and plan the vision to make a silk purse. Time is of the essence, so it seems, and becomes a measurement, an allocation, a commodity, an evaporating resource. Tools from experience include quick study, teach others, question source and data, diagnose before treating.

Deanology Lite

Why be a Dean, is said turning pale.

Who does it, what does it entail?

Opportunity knocks, only once or twice.

Anyone doing it needs to give and get advice.

Principles are key, as in discipline defining.

With confidence proceed, upbeat and no whining.

Start with preparation, performance is a must.

People and the person to enjoy and trust.

ARE YOU PREPARED BY PERSONALITY TRAITS AND VALUES TO BE A DEAN?

Positive	*Negative*
People are interesting	People are assey
Funds flow	Never enough money
Institutions improve	Like turning an aircraft carrier
Every day is a new beginning	Longevity is a dependent variable
Depend on delegation	Crisis management, damage control
Budgets are tools	Gaming
Planning is	Problems rebound
contained excitement	and carrousel
Officials offer support	Requests are attached
Expertise is necessary	Expert egos are large
79.9% approval rating	20.1% angry variable rating
Mentoring	Lost opportunities

Questions

A.   What preparation is essential for deaning?
   a.   Excellent education
   b.   Experience in the trenches
   c.   Record of accomplishments
   d.   Ready for on-the-job training
   e.   All of the above

B.   The role of the dean should be
   a.   Leader of the faculty
   b.   Manager of a multimillion dollar enterprise
   c.   Negotiator and fund raiser
   d.   A combination of traffic cop and cheerleader
   e.   All of the above

If your answer is "e," you are correct!

FACULTY AND STAFF RECRUITMENT

The dean, more than any other person, makes an impact on the institution through recruiting people to fill key faculty and administrative positions. Effective recruitment is well worth the time and effort. It is a most valued opportunity to enhance the institution with new blood and to sustain its academic growth through promotion and opportunities for outstanding internal faculty. Fortunately or unfortunately, turnover is high in academic positions. The unfortunate side is that the academic deadwood does not move, whereas the best and brightest frequently do, and as we all know such moves and re-recruitments become expensive. To give some idea of the magnitude of this opportunity and commitment over my seventeen years of deaning and being chancellor, consider that I have recruited people to fill seventy positions as chairs, associate or assistant deans, hospital administrators, or deans. This recruitment involved 3,000 applicants, 350 interviews, 500 search committee members, and innumerable phone calls. What is your level of enthusiasm for such a commitment?

COMPLEXYOMA

Theory The dean's job is complex, a magnetic attraction related to the complicated and comprehensive institutions served, and the complexity is growing. This benign tumor cannot be excised or irradiated, but we hope that it can be contained and prevented from progressing to malignancy and metastasis. A variety of therapeutic measures are evoked to process, solve, push forward, simplify, procrastinate and palliate compartmentalized issues.

Application The subject is far too complex to address briefly; however, the dean might wish to have a formula abbreviated to explain or reference the complicated enterprise.

$$\text{Complexity} = \frac{[\text{Big \& Small}]}{\text{Priorities}} \times \left(\frac{\text{pressure}}{\text{resistence}}\right) \times \left(\frac{\text{velocity}}{\text{time}}\right) - \left(\frac{\text{decision}}{\text{delegation}}\right)$$

- Modifier is blind luck

RE-ENGINEERING

Learning is lifelong, as we teach students, and as all deans know-before, during, and after deaning. The learning curve is inexorably elevating, increasing slope on day one and at stress and crisis points thereafter. The subjects change, however, and the variety of topics, issues, and problems remarkably diversify.

So one begins to notice a trend: the recall of a myriad of facts on patient care delivery diminishes, science and medical information marches on at increasing speed, and available time for study and practice is reduced. One resists the notion to attribute this trend to atrophy, apoptasis, or autoimmunity, but to invent a new expression - compensatory, partial delearning.

The relearning of medicine, challenging, exciting, and interesting, is generic, specialized, and chronologic. The tasks are several, in sequence and in parallel. Review to accentuate recall, find out what happened in the interim, add what is currently being produced, and collate all of the above. The reward is to improve one's capacity and skill in teaching.

Additionally, delearning and relearning occur at different rates, as is perceived and illustrated on the following graph.

Medical Re-engineering Aptitude Test

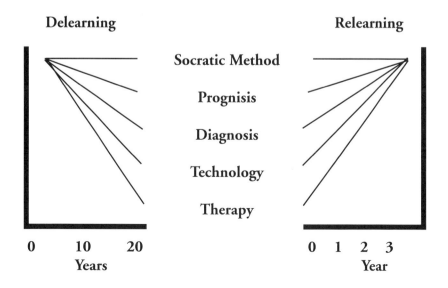

Delearning

Relearning

Socratic Method

Prognisis

Diagnosis

Technology

Therapy

0   10   20
Years

0   1   2   3
Year

USEFUL APHORISMS

- When you've seen one dean, you've seen one dean.
- What they don't know won't hurt them,
  but it sure as heck may hurt you.
- When the dean is traveling, everyone is planning.
- Advising and complaining take longer than reporting.
- Good information is worth more than a tome.
- A loyal colleague is like a pearl in an oyster.
- Quality is hard to define and easy to declare.

Almost on a daily basis, we see medical research in the lay press that contradicts previous research. For example, we hear that lipids are bad for your heart and then hear that serum lipids are good to prevent stroke. Like Lou Holtz, former Notre Dame football coach said, "We have rats that die of too much of something, and we have rats that die of too little of something. What we need are healthier rats."

23

> *T*here is one thing stronger than all the armies
> in the world and that is an idea
> whose time has come. Victor Hugo
>
> ～
>
> *A* good test of person's character is his behavior
> when he is wrong.

DECANAL REFLECTIONS

Douglas Skelton, MD

I attribute any success I have had as a medical dean to a love of medicine and a desire that others come to love medicine as much as I do. I expect that this is true of all successful deans. It is important, as well, to enjoy and to respect education and "the rules of the academy," which include collegiality, spirited debate, and faculty prerogatives (along with the dean and other university officials) for the business of education, i.e., selection of qualified students, curricular design, evaluation and promotion, and other activities. All of these activities are crafted into and around a multimillion dollar organization that, to run effectively, must use the skills of managing a business, organizing functionally, raising and accounting for revenue, negotiating contracts, and a myriad of other activities. There is nothing wrong with using good business practices to support and to sustain the academic enterprise. There is everything wrong - as we are seeing every day - with simply considering medical education and medical care as commodities to be bought and sold at a profit.

PRINCIPLES OF MANAGEMENT

Management principles are very important. I read the books and listen to the gurus. Here is what I remember from authors unknown.
- Some money costs too much.
- Money is a lousy way of keeping score.
- You can tell a lot about people by the way they handle these three things: a rainy holiday, lost luggage, and tangled Christmas tree lights.

PREPARATION TO BE DEAN

I believe that I was extremely well prepared for the Mercer deanship by a career path laden with academic, administrative, and political experiences, a career path that would benefit most deans but is not what most search committees desire in candidates. The lack of proper preparation requires many deans to do a lot of on-the-job-training, and while many adapt, others do not. During the more political (Governor's cabinet officer) portion of my career, I was asked why I was doing so well with the political infighting of state government. I replied, only partially in jest, that political infighting was easier in government than in academic infighting because you could see the knives coming. More seriously, of immeasurable importance to my efforts on behalf of Mercer have been the relationships developed during six years of government service (most of the power folks in Georgia are friends from those days), the unwavering support of Mercer's president, and quality staff and faculty colleagues. Many of the latter were selected by my predecessors, each of whom made unique contributions. Bottom line: quality academic medicine is a team sport.

LEADERSHIP

Teams have leaders, and leadership is the subject of legends - and some very boring presentations. Several years ago, Bill Curry, the former football coach at Kentucky, pulled it all together for me. He said, and I strongly agree, that leaders must never join the "fellowship of the negative" and they must keep negative thinking out of their organizations. I'm more indebted to Bill Curry for providing the best working definition of a leader I have ever heard, or at least the best I have remembered: "A leader must provide a consistent, powerful, positive present." This is the essence of the dean's leadership challenge, to be a consistent, powerful, positive presence for medicine, for medical education, for the medical school, for the academic center, and for the university.

Several sayings come to my mind:

• At 64, I've learned that most of the things I worry about never happen.
• Failures always blame someone else.
• Illustrate the consistency principle: If you are the leader and

you stop rowing, you shouldn't be surprised if everyone else rests, too.

• Consistency does not mean resistance or rigidity. What is required is consistency in support of change as a necessary ingredient of progress.

• The powerful aspect of leadership involves vision and risk taking, and the ability to make decisions rapidly and often under considerable stress.

• The movement notion is captured in "Lead, follow, or get out of the way."

• A person with big dreams is more powerful than one with all the facts.

• Powerful people don't fight battles if there is nothing to win.

• Many leadership failures have been caused by equating power with control and dominance. Academic institutions are not military organizations; much more give and take are required.

• Positive people are a joy to work with, and positive slogans abound. A few of my favorites are 1) Focus on your dreams, not your regrets; 2) One loss does not make a season; 3) Compare yourself to the best you can do, not the best others can do; 4) Being positive means not being too busy to say "please" or "thank you" or to compliment someone's work; and 5) Be nice to people on the way up, because you may meet them on the way down.

• I would modify Bill Curry's definition of a leader by adding the word ethical to the list of adjectives. Trust is such an important part of all relationships. Once breached, it is very difficult to restore. It was in my government days when I first heard a person described as having "round heels," i.e., being easy to roll over, not able to take a position and hold it. As the story goes, when Mark Twain was told, "You know George Washington could not tell a lie," Mr. Twain replied, "Yes, but I have a much higher standard than that. I could tell them - but I don't."

No one can hold a positive attitude all the time, but to be a leader it is necessary to hold one most of the time. I find Bill Curry's definition of leadership and admonition against negative thinking, buttressed by a few sayings and stories, helpful to me.

A SENSE OF HUMOR

A good sense of humor is also helpful. I find this especially true in dealing with recommendations for admission made directly to me. I always provide the person making the recommendation with some information, while stating that any final decision belongs to the faculty admissions committee. For totally unqualified applicants, I may use a sports analogy, e.g., "To get in the game one must at least be dressed out." But the best story involves a political friend who called with the following message, "This young man is absolutely the best applicant I have ever referred to Mercer." My return response was, "You are absolutely right. I've looked at the application. This one can read and write." "That bad, huh?" he said, and that was it. Humor can make unpleasant news more palatable and a stressful life more tolerable.

Medical deaning is exciting and challenging. Reflecting on my own career and on those of my colleagues, I believe that deaning appeals especially to those who enjoy "sliding down the razor's side of life" - for good causes.

---

*T*he dean went to a department faculty meeting expecting a large audience but only three faculty members showed up. Somewhat agitated, the dean asked the chair, "Did you tell everyone I was coming?" The chair said, "No, but I will find out who did."

24

> *Faculty crave order but defy authority.*

MEDICAL SCHOOL DEANING

Manuel Tzagournis, MD

$\mathcal{T}$here is probably no more diverse, interesting, or challenging job in medicine than being dean of a college of medicine. Most deans have the MD degree and can continue to participate in a favorite activity, whether that be patient care, teaching, or research. In truth, the bait of the job is an opportunity to have an important impact on the direction of programs of a major medical center. The Ohio State University is a state-supported (fortunately still not merely state-located) institution. It has the usual constituents—students, faculty members, donors, and alumni who have special rights over everything that goes on. As the land grant public institution, all tax-paying state residents and their elected officials have a sense of ownership as well.

At my university, good working relationships have existed among the colleges and hospitals. The camaraderie among deans and vice presidents of American academic medical centers is an unrecognized gem in getting ideas, solving problems, and receiving informal psychotherapy. My background as a faculty member, as an associate dean and medical director of our hospitals, was helpful in dealing with common problems of that period of time. Issues regarding practice plans, changes in the curriculum, affirmative action, research funding, increasing health care competition, and managed care emerged almost in succession from 1980 to the present. All deans faced these issues to a variable extent and dealt with them.

RECOLLECTIONS THAT MAKE GOOD STORIES

Each of these subjects is associated with memories and reflections that alternate between the stimulation of a challenging problem and heartburn. A favorite story that deans of medicine enjoy telling is, "I sleep like a baby, waking up every three hours to cry." Two recollections about deaning make good stories. The first is an example of a problem that blossomed into long-term benefits, and the second is an exercise between academic freedom and the reputation or credibility of the institution.

During the first few weeks of my tenure as a new dean, we

were preoccupied with repairing wounds from a practice plan dispute between faculty and the university administration. One morning the president called an emergency meeting to inform us of a dramatic budget reduction effective immediately. The State of Ohio was in a recession, and the governor legally had to balance the budget. He did so by making draconian, across-the-board reductions. That was the wrong time in history for a new dean to financially castrate a faculty struggling to catch its breath. I decided to draft a letter explaining our predicament to each of our living alumni (a very large constituency).

Remarkably, we had an unexpectedly good response from them. Serious fund raising was uncommon then because people believed that state taxes were "donation" enough. Not only did we receive a windfall, but later the president of our alumni organization, Dr. Dick Stager, initiated a "Hippocrates Club" asking for a minimum of $1,000 per year from alumni, faculty and friends to belong to a support group of the college. Several hundred Hippocrates members now regularly contribute to a very helpful fund-raising initiative at a public institution.

The second reflection deals with academic freedom and reasonable limits on claims about experiments conducted in the institution. Before the cause of AIDS was known, a basic science faculty member requisitioned a litter of "homosexual" pigs. How one determines whether a pig is homosexual remains unclear to me. Nevertheless, he was becoming less competitive in his discipline and was anxious to make a contribution to science. After some time he claimed that his experiments produced lesions that appeared similar to Kaposi's sarcoma. Several abstracts and offers to present his work at national and regional meetings were rejected. A manuscript was also rejected. One morning the "Lantern," the university's student newspaper read by most of the 50,000 students and many of the faculty members and staff, reported with page one headlines that an Ohio State University scientist had discovered the cause of AIDS. A short time later, with similar fanfare, this researcher reported rare and unusual bacteria in the pig lesions and claimed that the bacteria were also found in intravenous solutions and injectables sold by a quite reputable pharmaceutical company. A number of hemophiliacs who used the intravenous solutions began to call the medical center. When we heard that a private plane was flying to Ohio State carrying pharmaceutical executives from California, we felt compelled to distribute our own press release calling the findings unconfirmed, premature, and not yet scrutinized by peer review. The release did reduce calls from reporters and consumers and aborted a visit that was being planned by CNN. An internal review found that the "cause of AIDS" was a contaminant found in multiple sites in the investigator's own laboratory. Gradually, the story died, and the faculty member found another job some months later.

"So far so good" said the man who jumped from the 20th floor of the building as he passed the fifth floor.

THE DEAN AS LEADER

Every day something interesting happens, but there are satisfactions associated with being a dean of a college of medicine. Most American people respect that leadership position. Alumni and students look to the dean as the leader and representative of their academic heritage, and, deservedly or not, the dean gets accolades and reinforcement for many good things that happen in medicine. The dean is viewed much like the mayor of a city, enjoying the successes and fretting over failures and embarrassments. There are sad experiences: the faculty member who cannot understand or accept why tenure was denied; the student who is distraught at rejection of admission or dismissal from a long-sought-after career; the inability to get resources for a promising program. Obviously, the Dean must preside over the good things and manage the bad.

CHARACTERISTIC OF A SUCCESSFUL DEAN

People ask what it takes to be a successful dean. I don't know the answer, but there are some characteristics that are helpful, in my judgment.

> • Good interpersonal skills are probably more important than always making the right decision. Friendliness, attentiveness, understanding, and good humor are traits that enhance those skills.
> • The ability to communicate effectively to an audience is valuable because a dean cannot meet personally with all constituents.
> • Credibility is one characteristic that stands out. If one keeps personal and institutional promises and commitments, the word gets around. If you can't afford a recruitment package, don't make the promise, even at the cost of losing the candidate. If the dean can be depended on and trusted, the agenda gets accomplished even if it is "do more with less."

The faculty are often like those on the Mayflower: They stood on the verge of discovery of a new world but their thoughts remained with the old.

MANAGE CHANGE

The dean's most important task is to make and manage change. Virtually every present dean or vice president began a career in academic medicine when the enterprise looked much different than it does today. An incredible increase in research programs and full-time faculty practice marked the initial changes after World War II. Deans struggled to manage the growth of academic health centers, to develop practice plans, and to form large research organizations. More recently, health care costs and surpluses in health professionals and hospital beds stimulated different changes. Downsizing began, and managed care organizations gave birth to competition especially difficult for academic medical centers. Deans and vice presidents had to control and lead change so that academic health centers could continue to prosper and make the remarkable accomplishments expected of them

Changes were difficult in academia where everyone has input and a right to veto. I often refer to a letter written to President Andrew Jackson in 1829 and have quoted it in talks.

Dear President Andrew Jackson:

The canal system of this country is being threatened by the spread of a new form of transportation known as railroads. The Federal Government must preserve the canals for the following reasons:

1) If canal boats are supplanted by railroads, serious unemployment will result. Captains, cooks, drivers, hostlers, repairmen and lock tenders will be left without means of livelihood, not to mention the numerous farmers now employed in growing hay for horses.

2) Boat builders would suffer and tow-line, whip and harness makers would be left destitute. Canal boats are absolutely essential to the defense of the United States. In the event of the expected trouble with England, the Erie Canal would be the only means by which we could even move supplies so vital to waging modern war.

For the above mentioned reasons, the government should create an interstate commerce commission to protect the American people from the evils of railroads and to preserve the canals to posterity.

As you may know, Mr. President, railroad carriages are pulled at the enormous speed of fifteen miles per hour by engines which in addition to endangering life and limb of passengers, roar and snort their way through the countryside, setting fires to crops, scaring the livestock and frightening women and children. The Almighty certainly never intended that people should move at such breakneck speed.

Signed by Martin Van Buren, Governor of New York.

I guess the moral of that message is that, unlike Deans, future presidents of the United States can advocate the status quo.

---

*T*he dean received a letter from an angry faculty member who questioned not only the decisions that the dean had made but also the dean's integrity, honesty and ancestry. At the bottom of the letter, the dean wrote, "Some damn fool wrote this letter and signed your name to it," and returned it to the faculty member.

25

Every morning in Africa, a gazelle wakes up and knows that it must outrun the fastest lion to survive. Every morning in Africa, a lion wakes up and knows that it must outrun the slowest gazelle. Either way, every day, when the sun comes up, you'd better be running.

REFLECTIONS

Harry P. Ward, MD

Seven years as a Dean, and, now, 18 years as a Chancellor - and, finally, someone is asking me for advice!

THE SECRET OF SUCCESS IS
? ? ? ?

Reflections are so varied - truly from heights to depths, from successes to failures. I agree with the oft-quoted characteristic of "stamina" as the single important requirement for administrative leadership. I wish it were honesty, insight, enthusiasm, tolerance, intelligence, etc.; but, no, it is stamina, commitment and work. Most of us enter administration poorly prepared as measured by a structured academic preparation. We have been selected for achievements in research, clinical care, or education. Administrative responsibility has consisted of divisional or departmental leadership. All of us have shown the ability to work on committees and to recognize problems of the greater institution rather than our own individual needs. We are good "listeners" but like to talk. If we survive, our humor has pulled us through, and if we are truly successful, the achievements of others have made us look good.

PRECEPTS FOR A DEAN TO FOLLOW
INCLUDE THE FOLLOWING:

• Remember your first week of meetings. Virtually everyone who has called for an appointment will cause you long-term trouble. This fact gives you great appreciation for your predecessor - and teaches you an administrative rule: Hard problems are hard problems.

• Faculty members rarely read the same things that you do. This includes newspapers, Federal notices, interoffice communications, etc. They believe in the status quo, that there is no reason to change, and that "no one ever told me." A well-known dean who had served previously as chair of psychiatry was asked by a colleague, "Don't you miss seeing patients?" His response was, "I still am, but now they all have tenure."

• Be careful of numbers (Fig. 1). If I had a dime for every dollar we were going to save or to generate, I could start a new health science campus today. Don't trust your accounts receivable, and don't spend your accrued balance. Cash and reserves funded by cash are the only true dollars.

• These jobs are lonely. It is difficult and, perhaps, dangerous to keep close friendships with your institutional colleagues. You must maintain a level of objectivity without creating a barrier. This is a difficult line to maintain but organizations of over $500 million and over 6,000 employees demand a level of strong and evenly balanced judgment. So often, small problems end up at your door - but, even then, the resolution of these issues reverberates throughout the institution and sets the "tone" of your administration.

• Traditional hierarchical governance does not work in an academic health center. I was asked by the Chairman of the Legislative

Budget Committee, "Whom do you report to?" Although my response was greeted by laughter, it was accurate - "Everyone, Mr. Chairman." The constituency groups range from the president, the board of trustees, the governor, and the legislators to patient groups, parents, alumni, and employees. The most important group is the faculty! Without their support, you cannot serve. A true significant consensus must exist. Never implement a 51-to-49 vote - it will not work. Better still: never vote. A leader who is too far ahead of the army will be powerless. The mortality from "friendly fire" is probably the primary cause of the short tenure for these positions.

    • Your greatest successes will be the achievements of others. If you still need direct ego satisfaction, you probably should not be the dean or chancellor. Your job is to provide the environment, the internal milieu, for individual and group success. Leadership is guiding the institutional ship in the correct direction and providing the vision of the potential opportunities and risks. Implementation demands commitment of the greater majority. If possible, the administrator should "push" rather than "pull" the programs. You are guaranteed success when your council of chairmen or faculty senate "initiates" a strategic plan that unintentionally incorporates policies and, in some cases, phrases that you have planted and quietly pushed for months or years.

    • You are hired for your job at the institution. Regional and national participation is important and provides an easy access to experiences of other institutions. It helps you avoid errors and provides models that can be adapted to your own institution. In addition, you have a responsibility to share your experiences with your national colleagues for the same reason. But beware! National meetings have a potential to occur every week - and usually at exotic locations. Institutional balance is friable and needs constant attention. An absent leader, despite gaining national prominence, often has a short tenure in administration.

    • These jobs need a spouse. The social obligations are a requirement of the position - and it is most difficult to do them alone. The grace and thoughtfulness of a spouse ensure a successful evening. Not infrequently, your guests will prefer the company of your spouse to your own. Moreover, your spouse always remembers names, frequently brings a small gift, and follows up the evening with a note.

• Recruitment is a primary responsibility of these positions. Assistance for the recruit's spouse is critical in the final decision. This holds true regardless of whether the spouse is male or female. Your spouse can provide this assistance in selecting a house, choosing a school for the children, finding opportunities in the community, and providing access to compatible people. Medical centers are fortunate to have a mixture of faculty members, most of whom were recruited externally. The challenges are recognized, and your spouse can comfortably serve as the facilitator.

• Success is measured daily, and the "what have you done for me today" expectation is a faculty prerogative. I have been surprised at academic leaders who within a year after the opening of a specialized institute supported by a three-year institutional development program will complain that you are not supporting them. You are a bit like the Broadway actress - "only as good as your last hit."

• My final bit of advice, and maybe the most important, is this: do not personalize everything. This means success as well as failures. The true meaning of Osler's "Aequanimitas" may be most appropriate here. Stand back; be objective and slightly dispassionate. The institution is much greater than yourself, and it will survive your "watch." But it has been a great honor to have had the chance of doing:

"The best I know how, the very best I can. And I mean to keep on doing this down to the very end. If the end brings me out all wrong, ten angels swearing I had been right would make no difference. If the end brings me out all right, then what is said against me now will not amount to anything." Abraham Lincoln

A dean and his wife were walking to their hotel in Washington after a AAMC meeting when they saw a homeless man. The wife recognized the man as her former fiancee. As they walked on, the dean said to his wife that she must be happy that she married him, a successful physician and dean. She said, "Honey, if I had married the homeless man, he would have been a successful physician and dean."

26

> *B*e careful that your exercise program doesn't
> include jumping to conclusions.

THE DECANAL TIGHTROPE

Emery A. Wilson, MD

*U*pon accepting the position, most deans are somewhat intimidated and overwhelmed by the number and diversity of medical school projects, the complexity and magnitude of the budget, and the various requests that will come across their desks. The dean is responsible for a multitude of educational, research, and clinical issues, many of which are accompanied by background material as much as three inches thick that must be absorbed before the dean can be knowledgeable about the issues. Background study often requires much homework and many late nights and weekends so that the dean can converse intelligently about the subject. (Long hours spent on the job may impress your faculty members but will not impress your spouse).

BUDGETS

Medical school budgets can be complex and yet relatively simple. The sources of revenues and expenditures seem to be unending, but most of the budget is allocated to personnel and operating expenses. The budget is supposed to be a planning document that allocates resources to favored programs and projects. The preparation of the budget is also a negotiating process in which the needs of the medical school are positioned against requests from other academic units in the university, and the dean's role in justifying resources for a larger budget and additional programs is paramount. Most of the initial requests come from chairs who want to reconfirm commitments from the previous dean and who want to be first on the dean's agenda of new requests. Once all of the chairs have made an appearance in the dean's office (or, better yet, once the dean has visited all of the chairs), requests by chairs, faculty members, students, alumni, and others become a daily occurrence.

NEED FOR A CONFIDANT

It is important for deans and chairs to have a confidant - someone with whom issues can be discussed and argued without the information leaving the room. Newly appointed deans or chairs may have difficulty identifying a confidant within the institution and may need to recruit a valued and trustworthy colleague to serve this role.

A good friend doubles the joy and divides the pain.

SELECTING STAFF AND CHAIRS

The dean's most important responsibility is the selection of department chairs and medical school administrators - associate and assistant deans. The selection of both is important for different reasons. The effectiveness of the medical school's administrators reflects on the dean's ability and capacity to manage the school, and these administrators should have the personal skills necessary to relate to faculty members, students, and other university administrators. The academic background and the leadership and management skills of department chairs determine the overall direction of the medical school's programs and its ability to respond to environmental changes.

But the qualifications needed for effective department chairs are changing. In addition to maintaining academic standards, chairs must now be more responsible for the fiscal well-being of the department and the more direct management of the faculty members. Ideally, chairs should be accountants, organizers, social workers, and visionaries. Too much or not enough emphasis on any one of these attributes causes the chair to be ineffective. The same characteristics are necessary for deans. It may be difficult for one person to possess all of these characteristics, yet, in any organization, all of these attributes must be represented if the dean is to have an appropriate balance of the perspectives needed for the discussion of any issue.

The responsibilities of chairs have become extremely difficult and stressful, and chairs deserve the same level of support from deans that deans expect from their superiors. Deans should never talk to chairs or faculty members about other chairs except to praise them. If chairs need to be replaced, they should hear that message from the dean first and not from the rumor circuit.

Sometimes, the faculty members are right. Deans do not have to win every battle, and there are times when they should be quick to acknowledge a mistake and correct it. To the extent possible, deans should give credit and take blame. Much can be accomplished if one doesn't care who gets the credit. The perception of faculty members and students should be that the dean's overall interest is in the future of the institution and not in personal ambitions.

CHANGE VS. STATUS QUO

For the duration of their appointments, deans are continuously attempting to balance the school's need to change with the faculty members' desire to maintain the status quo. To create an exciting environment in which faculty members can excel, schools must constantly restructure their curricula, using current pedagogical methods, focusing research efforts to be competitive for external funding, and not only responding to the clinical environment but also taking the initiative to create the "product lines" or clinical partnerships necessary to maintain a patient base that is critical for clinical education and research. Meanwhile, most of the faculty members are reluctant to change. To this extent, Machiavelli was right: "The innovator makes enemies of all those who prosper under the old order, and only lukewarm support is forthcoming from those who would prosper under the new." The same is true with most of the faculty members. (Now I know that you have heard the stories about Mark Twain wanting to die in Kentucky because things happen there twenty years later, or the man who wanted to die in Chicago so that he could still vote, or the man who wanted to die in Israel because it has the highest resurrection rate in the world. But, when I die I want it to be in a faculty meeting, because there the transition between life and death can go totally unnoticed.)

This struggle to balance appropriate innovation and the comfort level of faculty members consumes an inordinate amount of the dean's time and has much to do with decanal longevity. For the first couple of years of the dean's tenure, the faculty members and chairs are willing to grant a honeymoon period during which the dean can usually do no wrong and any attempt to change the status quo is attributed to inexperience. The chairs are confident that they can out-last the dean anyway. Trouble usually occurs during the third year of appointment. Having developed a false sense of security because of success in the first year or two, the dean now has the confidence to attempt changes in one or both of the two areas that often lead to decanal self destruction: the curriculum or the practice plan (hence, the average duration of a dean's appointment at 3.5 years). Although administrative, management, and personal styles are important for implementing change, the most critical factor is support from one's superiors, the Vice President for Health Affairs and the president. If the faculty members and chairs can block initiatives by bypassing the dean in the administrative hierarchy, significant change is impossible, and the days of effective leadership for the dean are numbered. On the other hand, if the dean can weather the storms of change and main-tain the support of senior administration during the early years, the faculty members and chairs will come to realize that the dean has stay-ing power, and a relatively long tenure in the position can be expect-ed.

DECANAL LONGEVITY

From the dean's perspective, there are four important rules of decanal longevity.

• The first rule is to realize that no matter what the dean does, 20% of the faculty like it 20% hate it, and the others don't really care one way or the other. Actually, this rule is true of almost any controversial subject: abortion, health care reform, changing the curriculum, etc. As long as the vocally negative faculty can be confined to 20% or so, any change is possible. On the other hand, significant change is less likely as the opposing faction approaches 40%. One dean recently attempted to implement significant curriculum change by using a 52% faculty approval rating as a "mandate." He is no longer the dean at that institution.

• The second rule of decanal longevity is never to get more than three chairs "pissed off" at any one time.

• Third, the dean should be perceived by the faculty members to be honest, and if this perception can be achieved (or faked), the dean has it made. The new dean must understand that casual comments often take on extraordinary importance when made by the dean, and one learns to carefully select words when talking to faculty members and sometimes to chairs. Everyone begins to believe that "The sky is falling" when the dean says it.

• Fourth, deans should keep smiling, have a sense of humor, and be able to laugh, particularly at themselves. Being upbeat creates confidence that things are all right or soon will be.

---

*S*ome helpful suggestions when writing letters of reference:
   If you have to write a "Letter of Recommendation" for a fired employee, here are a few suggested phrases:

*For the chronically absent:
"A man like him is hard to find."
"It seemed her career was just taking off."

*For the office drunk:
"I feel his real talent is wasted here."
"We generally found him loaded with work to do."
"Every hour with him was a happy hour."

*For an employee with no ambition:
"She could not care less about the number of hours she had to put in."
"You would indeed be fortunate to get this person to work for you."

continued

*For an employee who is so unproductive that the job is better left unfilled:
"I can assure you that no person would be better for the job."

*For an employee who is not worth further consideration as a job candidate:
"I would urge you to waste no time in making this candidate an offer of employment."
"All in all, I cannot say enough good things about this candidate or recommend him too highly."

*For a stupid employee:
"There is nothing you can teach a man like him."
"I most enthusiastically recommend this candidate with no qualifications whatsoever."

*For a dishonest employee:
"Her true ability was deceiving."
"She's an unbelievable worker."

SECTION III
SUMMARY

27

*A young man approaches his grandmother
in the nursing home and asked,
"Do you know who I am?"
The grandmother replied, "No dear, but
if you ask the nurse at the desk, she'll tell you."*

COMPOSITION OF A DEAN

D. Kay Clawson, MD
Emery A. Wilson, MD

$\mathcal{T}$he evolution of the role of a medical school dean from a part-time administrator and clinician in the first half of this century to the business leader of an academic and clinical enterprise has been accompanied by an increasing turnover of deans. The increasing instability and lack of concrete planning associated with the increase in decanal turnover has had detrimental effects on both the position and the institution itself. The warm, friendly, congenial colleague selected by faculty, who was willing to sacrifice his/her own practice or research career in order to care for the administrative matters of the medical school was the prototype of deans early in this century. If the dean tired of performing the many routine tasks of the office, he could easily meld back into the faculty and another colleague was selected. In the post war era of medical school expansion with increases in class size, research portfolios and budgets, the role of the dean changed. The medical school became a multi-million dollar business conducted in a collegial environment. The dean, as the Chief Executive Officer of this enterprise, would have to manage the educational, research and clinical missions of the organization as well as plan for a rapidly changing environment. Hence, the dean has come to experience the same inflated expectations, stresses, and short term tenures common to leaders in the business world.

In their reflections, the deans write positively about their experiences and collectively portray what a dean does, the joys and sorrows of the position, the requisite personality and values needed as well as the inevitable conflict which occurs with day to day operations and with the management of change. These historical and personal perspectives provide us a unique opportunity to address the issues which are important in the selection and successful career of a medical school dean.

THE SELECTION PROCESS

Many of the deans who are not successful in the position can take solace in the statement, "It's not my fault; I shouldn't have been selected in the first place." The process to identify and select a dean with the characteristics necessary to provide the leadership and stability needed within our medical schools should be easy. Although the requirements for the position have changed, the traditional appointment process has not.

While many have called for a change in the process for the selection of a dean, it may be more important to look at the standards being used to judge the candidates' qualifications. Some search committees want an individual that is like what they aspire to be, while others look for someone who looks like them... but not quite as smart. Department chairs usually want a dean that is concurrent with them on academic values and prerogatives and with whom they are personally comfortable. As search committees pore over extensive curriculum vitae, the tendency is to look quickly at the number and quality of research publications as a top priority. This often proves to be a weakness in the selection process, for while it is helpful to be knowledgeable about research, writing papers and books provide little preparation for the position. Although there is value in using the curriculum vitae to determine if an individual has teaching, research and clinical experience, it says little about a person's administrative skills. If a candidate has been a department chair or if the vita indicates he/she has the respect of peers by having been appointed to a number of important committees (such as a dean's search committee), this information may be helpful in identifying candidates with appropriate attributes for a dean.

Perhaps we would all be well served by adhering to the Ten Commandments for Recruiting as written by Robert Pertersdorf:[1] Thou shalt keep search committees small, encourage advertising, not harass colleagues with needless letters, set a time limit for the search (including the time permitted for a candidate to reach a decision), obtain data selectively and not canvass the universe, encourage internal candidates, restrict visits to humane duration, avoid committee deadlocks, shun faculty stew, and if necessary feel free to search without a committee.

Not mentioned often enough is the value of an intelligent, hard working, supportive spouse. Support can come in maintaining a home life that decreases daily stress or it can be manifested by carrying out a variety of social commitments as a partner to the dean in these activities. The spouse is often important in recruitment of department chairs or key faculty members by providing professional, educational and social information about the community.

In the end, the selection of a dean is difficult but the process should focus more on the attributes and characteristics of the person rather than the individual's previous academic achievements.

CHARACTERISTICS OF A SUCCESSFUL DEAN

Someone once said that a college basketball coach should be a good recruiter, a good practice coach and a good game coach. He would be considered a good coach if he had one of these attributes, excellent with two and outstanding with all three. Very few coaches have been able to do all three and those that have, are legends. By analogy, if the characteristics of a dean could be limited to three, they would have to be:
• have vision and be able to communicate that vision,
• have the support of superiors, and
• have honesty and integrity.
If a dean had all three of these attributes, he/she would likely be an outstanding dean. Although very unlikely, it is possible for a dean to have only one of the attributes and still be somewhat successful. For example, if the dean enjoys unlimited support from superiors, he/she can do practically anything and maintain the position. If the dean has vision and is able to convince both superiors and faculty about new directions that the college should take, success and decanal longevity is likely. Or if the dean is so honest and has such integrity that he/she is trusted implicitly by superiors and faculty alike, continued support is also likely. Although these three characteristics are paramount, a number of other characteristics have been identified.

The unique perspectives of our contributors to this text provide us with an opportunity to identify characteristics which are likely to be necessary for a successful career. Table 1 identifies the more common characteristics of a successful dean and their importance rel-

Table 1
Characteristics of a Successful Dean

1. **Leadership and Administrative Skills** 52
2. **Honesty, Integrity, Fairness** 38
3. **Visionary Ability** 23
4. **Ability to Communicate, Speak** 22
5. **Political Skills** 19
6. **Knowledge of Finances** 15
7. **Cheerfulness, Sense of Humor** 15
8. **Relationship with Superiors** 14
9. **Ability to Select Chairs, Faculty** 14
10. **Ability to Delegate Responsibility** 9

ative to the number of times they were mentioned by our contributors.

Leadership and Administrative Skills

Everyone from the University President to faculty and students wants the dean to be a leader, someone he or she can look up to and trust. Unfortunately, the definitions that characterize a leader do not always support a consensus. Implicit in leadership is that there are also followers. The concept of having leaders and followers imply change in direction, values, structure and emphasis in the institution. Those who have chosen the academic life are often less action-oriented and want to explain or debate what is happening. Many want to argue the pros and cons of change with emphasis on social values. On the other hand, the university president, politicians and the public often demand change in a specific direction, commonly with an eye to the financial bottom line. And herein lies the basic conflict. The faculty want the dean to support a utopian academic environment, whereas others believe that the dean needs to show leadership by convincing the faculty of the need to change, to accept more patient care responsibility, to do more research, or to spend more time with students. Because of economic realities, the pressure will be to do more with less.

A job description which is known and understood by the dean and his/her superiors and constituents is necessary to define the position and the dean's role in the organization. It should define whether the dean has responsibility for all clinical activities or for only the academic programs of the college. Describing the needs of the position can help in the selection of the right person, which is critical to the success of the dean. Also, it may be helpful to distinguish clearly the responsibilities of the dean from those of the dean's superior, such as the Vice President for Health Affairs or the President.

To a great extent, a major responsibility of the dean as a leader is to describe reality and to provide alternatives to that reality. Faculty tend to be oblivious to political or economic issues happening around them. They are often interested in their own world of education or research and they believe the institution protects them from worldly or societal interference. It is often the responsibility of the dean to describe these events candidly and to lead the faculty in directions that will sustain an environment that is optimal for them to carry out their responsibilities.

One administrative skill that is necessary is timely decision making. It is frustrating to chairs and faculty to make a request and never receive an answer. Making a note and promising to provide an answer within a limited time reassures the faculty member or student that you are listening to his/her request and are willing to act on it. One should be careful not to be negative. It's often much easier to say no than it is to listen and conscientiously address the issue. Good deans should look for ways to say yes.

Management of the chairs and faculty is often an exercise in the management of conflict, and management of conflict usually results in compromise. A timely and definitive yes or no answer is always appreciated, even a no answer if adequately explained; but a compromise solution in an attempt to provide a win-win situation for both parties is the desired result when there is a conflict between two parties. Whether the dean likes it or not, he/she ultimately has to be a conflict manager and arbitrator, constantly looking for a compromise. Conflict is usually related to space or money. In some issues, especially space management, a faculty committee might be helpful in justifying the assignment of space, not to dodge the responsibility, but to assure fairness.

> *T*he ability to reconcile disparate elements in a sensible solution is the hallmark of a skilled politician — to do so with grace and vision is the gift of a statesman.

It is important to distinguish the concepts of leadership and management

- The manager administers; the leader innovates.
- The manager is an imitator; the leader is an originator.
- The manager maintains; the leader develops.
- The manager focuses on systems while the leader focuses on people.
- The manager relies on control; the leader inspires trust.
- The manager has a short-range view whereas the leader has a long-range perspective.
- The manager asks how and when; the leader asks what and why.
- The manager does things right; the leader does the right thing.

At times the dean must be a manager as well as fulfill the all important role of leader.

The dean should be careful not to allow a student or faculty member to put the "monkey" on the dean's desk when it's clearly a student or faculty problem. This is one of the most important points in time management. The dean can be overwhelmed with requests by trying to appear responsive and by removing the responsibility from someone else's shoulders. Chairs, faculty members and students should be encouraged to bring solutions as well as problems to the dean's office, and then they should be empowered to carry out those solutions, if possible, instead of leaving the problem with the dean.

The dean must have the intellectual and physical stamina to work long hours on a continuing basis and must do so for the support of the faculty and the school and not just to achieve personal agendas.

> "*The heights by great men reached and kept were not obtained by sudden flight, but they while their companions slept were toiling upwards in the night*". *Longfellow*

Whenever possible give credit and take blame. Take every opportunity to praise students, faculty and staff for any accomplishment. It's remarkable what can be accomplished when no one is interested in getting the credit for it. The most frightening thing for a dean is to recognize that he/she is responsible for hundreds of intelligent and enterprising students, faculty and staff while not always knowing what they are doing. If the dean makes a mistake or anyone in his/her organization makes a mistake, the dean is responsible and should take the blame. A difficult situation can often be diffused quickly. Most people understand that the dean is not really at blame, but by saying so, the discussion can turn from placing blame to doing what it takes to improve the situation. Being willing to take the blame for honest mistakes by faculty and staff can prevent them from suffering the embarrassment and endear the dean to them.

Being a dean may look glamorous, but it is tiring to attend all the holiday parties, alumni functions at home and away, numerous committee meetings and public appearances, and other functions ascribed to the responsibilities of the dean. Many deans tire of these perfunctory performances and withdraw to their offices or become engaged in national activities as an escape. A meeting at a resort site or at a distant city is never as stressful as a day in the office. A conscientious dean must recognize that, while it is appropriate to represent the school in various professional organizations, it may sometimes be used as an opportunity to avoid local responsibilities.

Two principal responsibilities of the dean are to describe reality and to effect change when needed. Most people will agree to change if there is data supporting it and if the change is incremental. Attempting change quickly in a collegial environment is dangerous. Major change requires time and significant faculty involvement. Change can be facilitated by internal champions or by external consultants. Often, faculty will accept a pilot program to determine if change is necessary when they might not have agreed to a definitive change.

The dean must also be aware of when the faculty has been overwhelmed with new projects and when the faculty needs a break. Sometimes it is important to step back from an issue to determine if it is really worth the battle. Occasionally, the dean will find that the issue is simply not as important as he/she originally thought.

Deans' Lament:
"I'm not allowed to run the train or see how fast it will go. I'm not allowed to let off steam or make the whistle blow. I can't exercise control or even ring the bell but let the damn thing jump the track and see who catches hell."

You can't make change using old mentality. If you keep doing what you have always done, you will get what you have always gotten.

Honesty, Integrity and Fairness

Ultimately, the ability of the dean to influence internal or external constituents will relate to how he/she is perceived as being honest and fair. It is all too easy to say one thing to one audience and something else to another, giving them a message that they want to hear in order to curry favor. A lack of trust will cause the demise of any dean. Hence, the portrayal of a straightforward and honest individual, one who has the ability to listen to others and receive information from all sides of an issue before making a fair judgment is essential. This is not an acquired attribute — at least not acquired in office. It requires years of consistent behavior, a willingness to admit mistakes and an administrative style that is open to constructive criticism.

A dean's integrity may well be his/her most important asset. As long as chairs and faculty believe that they will be treated fairly, they will come to realize that they can take risks and that they do not have to win every battle. This adage is also good for the dean to remember, that sometimes we win and sometimes we lose (as in budget negotiations), but the important thing is that we win the war and that the school is better in the long run. Occasionally, the chair or faculty member will say that the dean promised something that he/she doesn't recall. If possible, the dean should acquiesce to the requests rather than being perceived as reneging.

Visionary Ability

A dean should be a visionary, perhaps a dreamer, certainly an entrepreneur. As the English proverb states, "A vision without a task is a dream. A task without a dream is drudgery. A vision and a task are the hope of the world." This implies risk taking, embracing change and moving forward, but equally important is the ability to communicate the vision to others.

Some people simply don't have vision and it's not likely to be acquired once in office. In such cases, it is important for the dean to surround himself /herself with people of vision and to allow this inner circle to help establish and communicate the goals of the school. Department chairs can often serve this function if they can focus on institutional values. Chair retreats remove chairs from the day to day environment to think openly with less turf orientation. Overnight retreats with sufficient time for social interaction are also good for bonding.

A dean must have a vision for the future of the institution and must be able to clearly communicate that vision to students, faculty and staff, and alumni. This characteristic can not be underestimated in leading a medical school. In articulating the vision, the dean must first describe the reality of the current situation, present the ultimate goal which will resolve the current predicament, and describe the means by which that goal can be reached. In some cases, the vision relates to a day to day problem but usually the dean must have an overall vision for where the school is going and how to get there. The dean's vision must be compatible with that of the many constituents of the school.

In order to accomplish the vision, the dean is often the source of new ideas. Although this is usually considered an attribute, the dean should be careful not to burden the administrative staff and faculty with a plethora of ideas that are considered either frivolous or too numerous. In other words, the dean must be careful to select those projects which are important to the overall vision of the institution and not encumber the faculty and staff with busy work.

Ability to Communicate, Speak

The ability to communicate the school's vision, to interact with all of the school's constituents, to negotiate on the school's behalf, or to facilitate conflict resolution are key factors for the success of the dean. To be an effective public speaker is important. The dean is always in a position to represent the school of medicine and should do so at every opportunity. Often, the dean is called upon to present impromptu remarks and, although he/she may not be formally prepared, such occasions should be viewed as opportunities to represent the school. Deans are often called upon to make comments at social events and meetings. One way to organize comments, even when surprised, is to talk about some things that are happening in each of the three missions of education, research and clinical care that are appropriate to the context of the discussion.

The dean is not only a spokesperson for the school but is expected to be a spokesperson for health care in the region. There are many venues open to the dean to communicate the mission and accomplishments of the school, including presentations to legislative committees, opinion editorials, presentations to service organizations, etc.

Some conflict is inevitable between the dean and hospital administrators. It's not likely that the dean and hospital administrator will agree on everything because they have different missions and administrative styles. A hospital administrator oversees a corporate operation and frequently cannot understand why the dean cannot just "fire" an obstructive tenured faculty member. The dean and hospital administrator often have two levels of interaction — personal and administrative. An effective relationship between the two can be fostered if there is a good personal relationship underlying their negotiations as well as clear job descriptions for both. Ultimately, the dean and hospital CEO must understand that they must work together to develop the clinical enterprise.

The dean should have several routes of communication with faculty and staff - chairs council, conferences, faculty meetings, newsletters, etc. Even then, many faculty members will insist that they never heard of a particular issue before. Furthermore, the faculty will not always understand what you have said in the way you meant it. For example, one must be careful when "thinking out loud" because it is often interpreted as policy. One must be prepared to clarify and even rescind a statement when appropriate. Joking will often be taken seriously by faculty, so the dean must be careful not to underestimate the power of appropriate as well as inappropriate communication.

Political Skills

The dean must be an effective politician and indeed enjoy the political process. Politics is the art of getting along with other people when you don't necessarily agree with them, and encouraging them to do things important to you in exchange for things important to them. Scientists and scholars often find the political process offensive whether it be in government, business or academia. The success of a medical school frequently depends on politics which can be defined as the ability to accept compromise to realize some goal. A successful dean must know when to retreat on one issue, if only temporarily, in order to achieve success on another.

The dean must understand his/her role related to other administrators. The dean and faculty must recognize that the school of medicine is often perceived as the bully on campus because it is usually large and has more financial resources than other colleges. Establishing a personal relationship with other deans can help build political support within the institution. Political skills are important when dealing with superiors - Vice President, President, Board of Trustees - so as not to undermine their effectiveness and positions within the institution.

Knowledge of Finances

The need for financial skills cannot be minimized. A medical school is a multimillion dollar company. Most deans have no experience with budgets of this magnitude. In the first month following appointment, the dean should seek to understand the budget, revenues and expenditures, and the amount of fund balances available for flexible use. A scrupulously honest and compulsive financial director is an absolute must. This person also tends to have significant institutional memory and keeps an accurate log of promises and commitments requiring financial support.

More and more, the dean is involved in the language of business and the business of medicine. Business terminology is used in the development of group practice activities, planning research buildings and many other medical school functions. Familiarity with business terminology and, if possible, even a master's in business administration would be helpful in the preparation to be a dean.

The most important financial document for a medical school is the annual budget, and the dean must become involved in the budgetary process. The budget is a document that not only specifies the assets, liabilities, revenues, expenditures, and fund balances; it is also a planning document which delineates the programs considered to be most important by the school's administration as signified by the allocation of funds to support those programs. A strategic plan, developed with the involvement of faculty and chairs and appropriately updated on a periodic basis, is an important tool in identifying the programs which will require funding through the budgetary process. The budgetary process is usually a negotiating process. The dean must negotiate with the President or Vice President for Health Affairs for programmatic funding that is available to other academic units as well. An important part of this negotiating process is to align the school's programs with those programs that have been identified by the President and Vice President through discussions that have taken place during the year. Presidents favor university wide programs and vice presidents favor medical center programs, so the savvy medical school dean will align college programs with those of the rest of the institution in order to get additional funding.

Most universities are preparing for what has been called a major transfer of financial resources from one generation to another. It is predicted that over three trillion dollars will transfer to a younger generation in the next five to ten years. Universities are preparing for a major increase in development funds, and medical school deans should be involved in this planning. It helps to be a good fund raiser, but it's uncomfortable to ask people for money. It becomes easier when the dean is asking for money for the institution rather than for his/her own program. It is also easier if the dean has made a significant contribution before seeking contributions from others. Although surprise gifts of major proportions are not uncommon, most development funds are generated from people who become involved in something that they are interested in. Involving alumni, prominent patients, and community leaders in medical school activities is the best way to build a development office. 90% of the funds raised come from 10% of the people, and those who have given significant amounts of funds in the past are more likely to do so in the future. Therefore, the dean must play a role in continuing to nurture major donors as well as involving potential donors in the activities of the college.

Cheerfulness, Sense of Humor

High on the list of personal characteristics is a cheerful disposition coupled with a sense of humor, the ability to not only enjoy humor but to be able to laugh at one's self as well. Faculty morale reflects that of the dean. If the dean doesn't present an upbeat approach, this is likely to reflect on both subordinates and superiors and lead to a concern that things may not be well. Therefore, it is important for the dean to demonstrate a sense of well-being. A well timed vacation to get away from the daily requests and harassments may be necessary. Appropriate humor, especially if it is self deprecating, can help to dissipate bad news. A person with a cheerful personality will inspire others and create an environment that is pleasant to work in and likely to be constructive. Coupling cheerfulness with a sense of humor makes it easy to engage people in comfortable conversation and work through stressful situations by diffusing hostility.

On the other hand, the dean must be careful not to denigrate something that is valuable to the faculty. If the dean questions whether a joke should be told because of its potential for doing harm, it's better not to tell it. No humor is better than inappropriate humor.

A dean seems to be surrounded by people but has no friends. Most of the dean's time is consumed by school activities and this often precludes the development of friendships within the school in order to avoid partiality and outside the school due to the lack of time and interests. Again, an understanding and supportive spouse is a valuable friend and confidant.

Relationship with Superiors

It is important to have the support of superiors - President and Vice President - on any major decision before acting, such as requesting a major allocation of funds, seeking a new program or removing a chair. Frequent and substantive communication is the key to support of superiors. Sometimes legal counsel is also important.

Again, taking responsibility for things that go wrong as well as credit for things that go right strengthens the relationship of the dean with his/her superiors. The dean will not agree with every decision of the President or Vice President and, certainly, the dean should express a differing opinion when necessary. But once a decision is made, even if the dean disagrees, the dean should understand that it is an institutional decision that may be based on information available only to superiors. If the dean cannot support the decision, then he/she should consider resigning from the position. At no time should the dean undermine the authority of the President or Vice President. The dean would never appreciate the faculty or chair bypassing him/her, so the dean should remember never to bypass his/her superiors.

Ability to Select Chairs and Faculty

The greatness of any medical school rests with the quality of its faculty and students. Quality chairs and faculty tend to attract additional quality faculty members and students which are important in building the reputation of the institution.

The criteria mentioned above for the selection of the dean are also appropriate in the selection of chairs. A chair may be academically brilliant, generate thousands of research dollars or have a string of publications, but not be able to administer a department. Although the academic "tickets" are important considerations, they should not be the only criteria. The same leadership, administrative, interpersonal, visionary, and communication skills mentioned above are needed to lead each academic unit.

In the search for chairs, most candidates want to know what the school is going to do for them in the way of salary, space, and start up package. A smart dean is more interested in employing the chair who can articulate what he/she is going to do for the school. A few outstanding chairs in department leadership can set the direction of the school and assure success in its mission. It helps to have appointed the chairs because they are then more likely to be aligned with the dean's philosophy and vision for the school. Chairs, like other administrators, often become less effective with time. After ten or twelve years, serious consideration should be given to changing the department's chair unless the chair continues to provide exceptional leadership. It helps to establish this policy early in the dean's tenure so that the chairs do not expect life-time appointments.

Being a chair today is difficult, perhaps the most difficult job in academic medicine, especially when academic budgets are tenuous. Therefore, the dean should support chairs to the extent possible and should never undermine them. The dean should support chairs in the same way that the dean expects support from his/her superiors. Of the major responsibilities of chairs — direction of academic programs, research, clinical care of patients, mentoring, and communication — failure to communicate important information from college administrators to faculty and vice versa tends to lead the list of shortcomings. Therefore, the dean must continue to communicate directly with the faculty through faculty meetings, newsletters, etc.

When a chair has lost the confidence of the dean and/or the faculty, the chair must be replaced. The symptoms of an ineffective chair are usually a disgruntled faculty, faculty leaving for other positions or for private practice, inability to recruit, and/or poor budgetary management. Although most chairs understand that they serve at the pleasure of the dean and often state that they would readily step down if asked, they seldom do. Most chairs would prefer to blame external influences - managed care, the dean, or others - instead of candidly assessing their own performance. When possible, the dean should help the chair save face by allowing him/her to resign. One approach might be to inform the chair that replacing him/her is necessary, giving the reasons, and then discussing how the change in departmental leadership should occur. Ideally, the chair would have two to three months to interact with the faculty, explaining the increasing stress of administration, and finally announcing to the faculty that he/she is stepping down. The dean should be aware that the chair may attempt to generate support from the faculty, President, Vice President for Health Affairs, Board of Trustees, legislators, and others, which further reinforces the need for the dean to communicate the reasons for change to superiors and obtain their support prior to taking action.

Ability to Delegate Responsibility

Everyone wants to see the dean; everyone wants to talk with the dean; everyone wants to hear his/her opinion. With the multiple responsibilities and decisions that must be made in a major medical center today, this is not only impractical but impossible. The only way to be an effective dean is to be able to delegate effectively and efficiently. The dean must be able to delegate responsibility with attendant authority and then support the decisions of those who have been given the authority even though at times, the subordinate may not have done exactly what the dean would do. The dean must have a comfort level with the people he/she has chosen to receive this delegated authority and they must understand their responsibilities for bringing tasks to successful closure. A person who is by nature suspicious or insecure and who wants to know all of the details before an action can be taken will be very uncomfortable delegating authority and soon will be swallowed up in so much daily activity that he/she will be unable to function in the role.

One should be careful to distinguish delegating from dumping. Delegation consists of assigning responsibility and periodically evaluating how it is being managed. Dumping relates to forcing a colleague to do something we do not want to do ourselves; it is never appreciated. Some things simply cannot be delegated. Students, faculty and alumni want the attention of the dean and when possible, they should get it.

WHAT DOES THE DEAN DO?

The dean must have a strong work ethic. Table 2 lists a sampling of the activities in which the dean is involved during a representative year. These are scheduled meetings and do not reflect the times that the chairs and faculty drop by to chat or the time spent in casual conversation in the hallway. Few understand or appreciate the magnitude of these activities. Obviously, with such a schedule, the dean will have a superficial knowledge of many issues but an in-depth knowledge of only a few, which makes delegation of responsibility and reliance on key staff members all the more important. The wide range and number of requests for the dean's time and attention can actually divert him/her from the major responsibilities of the position. From time to time, the dean's staff and schedule require reorganization in order to fulfill the job requirements and still meet the expectations of the faculty, students, and others. A dean's time is seldom his/her own. Time management, which has become an important administrative

Table 2
What does The Dean Do?

Internal Meetings (per year)		Annual Performance	
Council of Chairs	12	Evaluations	32
Clinical, VA, Group Practice		Budget Hearing	26
Plan Meetings	55	Talks, Presentations, Updates	196
Associate/ Assistant Deans	56	Breakfast, Luncheons,	
Student Groups	23	Dinners, Receptions	255
President / Vice President	56	Faculty Meetings	23
Individual Chairs	109	Nights on Call	12

State / Nation Activities
 (meetings per year)
 AAMC, AMA, Licensure
  Board, State Assn. etc.   26

Community Activities
 Local Medical Society,
  Boards   30

Avg. Number of Meetings per day   7.1

Avg. Pieces of Mail per day   30

skill and which can be learned, is necessary to carry out the responsibilities of the job. For example, delaying a decision unnecessarily only prolongs the task and the time related to it. Major decisions should not be made in the hallway. Although many meetings are associated with meals, most people are only interested having the dean present, not how much he/she eats. An executive assistant who can diplomatically triage faculty, students, visitors, and mail is critical to a smoothly operating dean's office. Sometimes mail placed in a stack on the desk does not seem nearly as important two or three weeks later as it did the day it is received, and it can be more easily discarded.

Part of the dean's job is to manage by walking around. Meeting and spending time with faculty and students, learning what they do, and empathizing with their plight is an important means of communication. Unfortunately, the longer the dean is in office and the more responsibilities that are acquired, the less likely he/she has the time to become directly involved with these constituents. Because of the importance of such activities and the effectiveness of this type of communication, time must be set aside in the schedule for this.

Although the dean may feel a need to be omnipresent, vacation time is important to restore some perspective to the dean's role and interactions with others. Although diversity of the responsibilities in the job is sometimes an advantage, the activities, the confrontations, and the inability to please everyone eventually impairs judgment and a sense of well-being. There's nothing like a walk on the beach, a cabin in the woods, or a drive across country to restore perspective. Periodically, during these escapes, it is helpful to remember why one was selected in the first place - personal relationships, a ready smile, a willingness to listen - to clear the mind and restore priorities.

THE CHANGING ROLE OF THE DEAN

The future of academic medicine lies in the production of leaders who can clearly articulate a vision for the institution to allow the faculty to do their jobs as creative investigators and exciting teachers. Some universities and organizations have designed a spectrum of courses to determine if a faculty member is interested in administrative medicine and to teach the administrative and management skills necessary to be successful in leadership positions such as chair, associate dean, or dean. The University of Kentucky, for example, has three courses taught by the business school in conjunction with the medical center, which include a one week overview of medical economics, management, leadership and accounting; a certificate program, which includes four courses on these subjects in greater detail; and the Master's in Business Administration with an emphasis in health care. Such a range of courses allows young faculty members to determine if they are interested in administration and how far they wish to proceed. The Association of American Medical Colleges also has a number of short term courses designed to prepare faculty for administrative positions. In the future, deans are more likely to come into the position better prepared with business backgrounds and, therefore, more likely to be successful in the position.

Perhaps it is time to embrace the decanal philosophy of the dean as an academician, instead of the dean demanding more responsibility, more control, and assuming more the role of a manager. In this philosophy, the dean would stress leadership in achieving academic success while leaving to another individual the role and function of the chief executive officer of the patient care organization. Some academic medical centers have already split the traditional decanal responsibilities for academic programs and patient care between two individuals. In some cases, the clinical organization is administered by the Vice President for Health Affairs and the dean is responsible for academic programs. Alternatively, the dean has assumed the responsibility for clinical programs and has assigned the academic programs to an executive dean or vice dean. The implication, of course, is that the job has become too big for one person to manage effectively, and divided responsibilities are more likely to be commonplace.

In the future, the dean is not likely to have the authority that is now inherent in the position. Faculty will demand more of a voice in the management of the medical school and clinical faculty and chairs will take more responsibility for the group practice concept. Although these actions are necessary to engage and empower the faculty in clinical and other academic activities, the dean must willingly relinquish some power and support the concept in order for it to happen. In the same way patients want to be involved in their own care, faculty want to have a voice in their own destiny. Deans who are unwilling to relinquish such power will find it difficult to administer in tomorrow's health care system. On the other hand, those who can continuously adapt to a changing academic and clinical environment, seeking out the involvement of faculty and staff, are more likely to be successful.

MEDICAL SCHOOLS OF THE FUTURE

Many physicians would say that the period from 1960 to 1990 was the golden age of medicine. Physicians were independent, controlled the vast spectrum of patient care, were highly respected by patients and society, and were reimbursed handsomely for their knowledge and skills. The same perspective may be true for medical schools. During this era, the Flexnerian medical curriculum remained unchallenged; research discoveries funded by federal agencies, foundations and industry were unprecedented; and the passage of Medicare and Medicaid legislation in 1965 allowed medical schools to generate so much clinical income that some of it was readily used to subsidize education and research. During the past decade, that has all changed. A massive increase in medical information has forced a change in the way that medical students learn; funding for research has become much more competitive; and the regulatory changes and cost-containment expectations of government and industry have reduced clinical revenues and severely limited the capacity to cross subsidize other medical school activities. In the next decade, some medical schools will find it difficult to survive financially, and medical school deans will be called upon to make significant changes in the current academic paradigm.

The changes which will occur in medical schools will be somewhat evolutionary in nature. With the changes in managed care, clinical revenues and clinical faculty salaries will remain the same or decline even as the clinical work load increases. The clinical faculty will be asked to work harder for less money, and they will demand to be compensated appropriately. In order to determine which faculty members are actually working harder to generate more clinical revenues, their productivity must be measured. When clinical faculty members realize that teaching medical students is jeopardizing their capacity to generate a higher salary, they will demand compensation from medical school sources, and measures of teaching productivity will have to be developed. The same will likely be true for researchers. Consequently, clinical revenues will be used to pay faculty for clinical activities, extramural research funds will be used to pay for research, and tuition and state funds will be used for educating students. Productivity measures in education, research, and clinical care will be used not only as a basis for compensation but will provide objective measures of overall faculty performance. This is the rationale for mission-based planning and budgeting. The traditional, triple-threat academician in medicine will be a thing of the past; and in order to be judged as successful, faculty members must concentrate most of their efforts in a single mission. As a result, the whole concept of tenure will be challenged.

The dean's role in the future will be to protect the vestiges of academic medicine and to provide an environment where faculty can excel. Implementing change will be difficult enough, but dealing with what some have called "reform without change" may be more challenging. New ways of doing business may be initiated, but chairs and faculty have a tendency to continue to perform in the traditional academic mode. At some point, the turf orientation mentality will have to give way to multidisciplinary approaches in education, research, or clinical care in order for the medical school to be successful in the new era.

Education

During this decade, the Flexnerian, lecture dominated curriculum has been giving way to more active student learning and an introduction to newer pedagogical techniques. These changes are encouraged by the Liaison Committee for Medical Education, and deans should familiarize themselves fully with the "musts" and "shoulds" in the accreditation standards. As technology continues to develop, more sophisticated pedagogical techniques such as virtual reality or virtual immersion for gross anatomy, surgery, intensive care simulations, etc. will be available for educational purposes. Of some concern are the costs of these new pedagogical methods, especially when the ability to cross-subsidize will be more limited.

The cost of medical education in the future will continue to rise as will tuition. The amount of tuition each student must pay was less of a factor several years ago when tuition was less, often subsidized with scholarships or low interest loans and physician incomes were relatively high. As medical schools continue to increase tuition and fees, medical school expenses will outstrip scholarships and student debts will continue to grow. Relatively lower incomes for physicians in the future will make it much more difficult to repay loans and may have an impact on the number of qualified students admitted to medical schools, as well as specialty selection.

How many faculty members do we need to teach medical students? This question will become more important when medical school revenues decline. The number is probably fewer than we realize. Some have suggested that only teachers and not researchers should be involved in medical education and have control of the medical curriculum. Financial restraints and necessary changes in the organizational structure may cause this to occur, although the presence of basic and clinical research is important to the overall education of medical students and is an accreditation standard.

If team care is going to be important in the future care of patients then team teaching and learning is a prerequisite. Physicians will be more involved in the multidisciplinary care of patients, and the virtues of working with other health professionals will become more important in the medical curriculum. Again, the costs of multidisciplinary teaching are a concern.

Research

Medical research is highly regarded by the people of this country and there is increasing interest in research developments. Surveys by Research America have demonstrated that most people believe that research is important and the vast majority think that medical research is the most important type of research. Congress also believes that medical research is important and has continued to support medical research funding through the National Institutes of Health and the National Science Foundation.

In the post-war era, medical research has evolved from research using whole animals, to organ culture, to tissue culture, to cell culture, and, finally, to molecular research. With the completion of the human genome project, the findings of research performed at the molecular level will be translated to the bedside, and there is likely to be more whole animal, clinical research concentrated on transferring the knowledge we have obtained from molecular experiments to human diseases. Research in the next decade is likely to be focused on genetics and transplantation and the prevention of rejection reactions. The economic impact of medical research and its relationship to industry both in the development of new technology and new companies makes continued research funding relatively secure in the near future.

Medical research is likely to be concentrated in fewer and fewer medical schools. Although medical research will continue to be valued by Congress and the American people, many schools will not be able to afford the research infrastructure necessary to be competitive for funding. A school must have good researchers in order to recruit good researchers, and significant resources in space, technology and start up funds will be necessary to be successful. Perhaps only one-half of the medical schools will have significant peer-reviewed extramural funding. If this occurs, what is the role of those schools incapable of obtaining such funding? All medical schools should be capable of performing quality clinical research, and medical schools will develop systems to conduct clinical research more efficiently. Clinical research will be considered also as an important alternative stream of revenue. Another role for both research and non-research oriented schools will be to transfer new medical information and technology to the practicing community. Even schools not heavily involved in medical research can improve health care in their respective service areas by being the first to use new information and technology and by educating local practitioners.

Clinical Care

For the past decade, the cost of health care has been the major issue; now, it's fraud and abuse, and the future is likely to concentrate more on quality of care. Even as interest in alternative medicine rises, medical care will be more evidence based and there will be more emphasis on patient service and satisfaction. Health care will continue to be market driven but the extreme methods introduced by for-profit, managed care companies will be moderated by federal and state statutory regulations. The profession and the American public will be more conscious of and suspicious of regulations because more regulations beget more investigations; eventually, there will be an attempt to decrease administrative paperwork in deference to caring for the patient.

Present and future well-being of medical schools, as well as the medical profession, will be driven by medical technology. Where would we be today if the techniques for angioplasty, CAT-scan, or MRI had never been developed? As long as medical schools continue to be at the cutting edge of medical technology, they will be perceived as necessary and will prosper.

Of future importance to medical schools will be progress toward universal coverage. Medical schools care for a large number of indigent patients or patients with no insurance, and this number is likely to increase without government support. In other words, this country already has universal access through its medical schools and teaching programs, and improvement in coverage is necessary to ensure that such access will continue to be available in the future. Approaches to universal coverage are likely to be incremental (like all significant changes). The government attempt to restructure health care and provide universal coverage in 1994 was a failure because it attempted too much too soon. Additional children will be provided care through the 1997 Children's Health Improvement Program and there will be other attempts to provide care for patient populations which are not currently covered. In general, incremental support for any segment of the population will benefit medical schools.

What is the teaching hospital's role in tomorrow's health care system? It will likely be a large intensive care unit for patients with complicated or uncommon diseases. It will also be the center for quaternary care, where the latest technological advances are developed and tested. Other community hospitals or hospital systems will improve their credibility through affiliation with teaching hospitals which fulfill this role. The teaching hospital will reap benefits from such affiliations by gaining sites for teaching and the provision of more routine care.

The dean and the teaching hospital director must be responsible for maintaining an environment which is attractive to clinical faculty. Traditionally, physicians have selected academic medicine for the opportunity to teach, do research, and be creatively productive. With increasing demands for clinical productivity and the generation of clinical revenues, the clinical academic environment is becoming much more like that of private practice, often with lower compensation, so the clinical faculty see no reason to stay. Systems must be developed and improved within the medical school and teaching hospital environment which continue to stimulate the academic curiosity of the faculty and which make it easier to practice in an academic setting.

WHEN IS IT TIME TO QUIT?

Like other administrators, deans often find it difficult to acknowledge when to step down, and this may be true for deans with short as well long standing tenure. In general, reasons for relinquishing the position fall into four categories: a) promotion or retirement; b) when "everything" is accomplished; c) when effectiveness is lost; and d) when superiors say so.

Many deans retire in the position or they are promoted to vice president or even university president. Others are "promoted" when they move to administrative positions of national organizations, foundations, or agencies. In most cases, these deans have been effective administrators, but the opportunity for advancement superseded their willingness to remain as deans.

There comes a time in any leadership position when one has accomplished all that he/she can. This is often true also of medical school deans. The dean should be content with carrying out accomplishments to the best of one's ability and creating a firm foundation for the next dean so that those accomplishments can be sustained and developed further. Most people think they should retire or resign about two years before other people think they should. As the Bible says, there is a time to reap and a time to sow. If one leaves too early, he lives to regret it; if he leaves too late, others live to regret it. Of course the difficult decision is to determine when one has accomplished all and when one has lost effectiveness.

It must be difficult for the dean to determine when he/she has lost effectiveness. Ironically, the faculty know almost immediately. Like any other disease process, there are signs and symptoms of lost effectiveness: when one avoids confrontation, when it becomes important to be popular, when there is fear of losing the job, when one escapes by spending more time away from the school in national activities, when one is no longer interested in stimulating change, when one tires of fighting, when things become too easy, when one becomes persistently angry at the "administration", and when there is consistent lack of support from superiors. The perceived lack of support must be consistent because all administrators must understand that they win some and lose some but that successful deans win more than they lose over time. Finally, as in any hierarchical system, the dean answers to his/her superior, who may recognize that the dean has accomplished all that he/she can, has lost effectiveness, or simply does not have an administrative style or personality that is consonant with the superior.

CONCLUSION

Can the personality and personal characteristics of an individual determine success in the role of medical school dean? From the writings and reflections of our contributors, it would appear that they can. Perhaps personal characteristics even provide the basic underpinning of what is true leadership. While personal characteristics should be carefully reviewed by search committees and those responsible for appointing deans, it is important that individuals who view themselves as potential deans also should ask, "Do I have the personal characteristics necessary to be a successful dean or should I pursue other opportunities in academic medicine?"

Countless deans have attempted to work in the complicated, ill defined, interdependent world of education, research, patient care, politics, and societal expectations. Some have left voluntarily in frustration. Some have been quietly removed; others summarily fired. But many have accepted the challenges and responsibilities, have worked within the confines of the system, and have moved the institution forward to even greater excellence. In the process, they have found tremendous personal and professional satisfaction, and, as a result, they have created within themselves their own golden era of medicine.

Reference:
1. Petersderf, R.G., "The Academic Mating Game," *New Eng. J. Med. 298*: 1290-1294., 1978

"One should not look back in anger, nor forward in fear, but around with awareness." Senator Nancy Kasselbaum, Kansas

"It doesn't matter what you think or what I think. When history is written it will be what you do and what I do."

Governor A. B. "Happy" Chandler, Kentucky

Qualities for Success

Sincerity
Personal Integrity
Humility
Courtesy
Wisdom
Charity

Dr. William Menninger